A Native's Guide To Chicago's

NORTHWEST SUBURBS

Martin A. Bartels

First Edition

Lake Claremont Press
4805 North Claremont Avenue
Chicago, Illinois 60625
http://members.aol.com/LakeClarPr

A Native's Guide To Chicago's Northwest Suburbs
by Martin A. Bartels

Published August 1999 by:

 Lake Claremont Press
4805 N. Claremont Ave.
Chicago, IL 60625
773/784-7517; LakeClarPr@aol.com
http://members.aol.com/LakeClarPr/

Copyright © 1999 by Martin A. Bartels
First Edition

ISBN: 1-893121-00-3: $12.95 Softcover
Library of Congress Catalog Card Number: 98-62508

Publisher's Cataloging-in-Publication
(Provided by Quality Books, Inc.)

Bartels, Martin, 1960-
 A native's guide to Chicago's Northwest suburbs /
by Martin Bartels. — 1st ed.
 p. cm.
 Includes index.
 LCCN: 99-62508
 ISBN: 1-893121-00-3

 1. Chicago Suburban Area (Ill.)—Guidebooks.
 2. Chicago Suburban Area (Ill.)—History.   I.
Title.

 F548.68.N8B37 1999   917.73'110443
                        QBI99-1039

**Printed in the United States of America by United Graphics,
an employee-owned company in Mattoon, Illinois.**

To the late Mrs. Dorothy Osborne,
whose teachings at
Summit County High School
serve as eternal inspiration.

Also thanks to
Paul and Regina Bartels,
David and Peggy Kirkpatrick,
and most especially,
Robin,
for unconditional support and encouragement.

CONTENTS

ACKNOWLEDGMENTS
AND
SOURCES

The author wishes to thank the many people who offered invaluable assistance, insights, and recollections in the research of the book.

Much of the information contained within this book was obtained with the assistance of the local historical societies, museums, and chambers of commerce, the names and addresses of which are contained herein.

Community statistics were also obtained from the U.S. Census Bureau, the Northeastern Illinois Planning Commission, and various village government offices.

Finally, the production of this book would not have been possible without the help of Sharon Woodhouse, Brandon Zamora, Susan McNulty, Ken Woodhouse, Brandei Bell, Bill Lane, and editor Bruce Clorfene.

A Native's Guide To Chicago's

NORTHWEST SUBURBS

GETTING STARTED

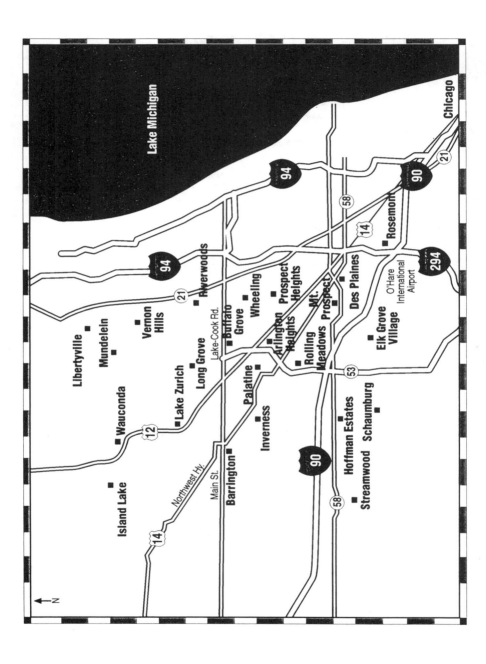

THERE'S LIFE IN THE SUBURBS!

As entertainment editor for the northwest group of Pioneer Press Newspapers, I've often been confronted with the stereotype that my territory must be among the most banal in all of journalism. After all, with a city as vibrant and culturally appealing as Chicago just minutes away, what on earth could there possibly be worth doing in the suburbs?

I'm happy to say the disdain is entirely unwarranted. It may have been true that, once, the suburbs were sleepy little hamlets serving only as rest stops for those commuting to jobs, and presumably, social lives, in the city. Even within the past decade, all of that has changed dramatically.

A Brief History

For the purposes of this guide, the Northwest Suburbs of Chicago are those villages that border Interstate 90 (the Northwest Tollway) or Route 14 (the Northwest Highway). There are a few exceptions: notably, Libertyville, Mundelein, Vernon Hills, and Lincolnshire, most of which rest along the "north corridor" of Milwaukee Avenue.

The area of I-90 that includes most of these villages is often referred to as the "Golden Corridor," a term that cropped up in the mid-1980s when area politicians fully realized the potential for local economic development.

The roadways themselves are important to the development of these towns. In pre-19th century northern Illinois, most of what are, today, major thoroughfares, were then trading routes for the Native American tribes that populated the region.

The settlement of the region is shadowed by the same bittersweet history of tragedy and courage that marked the westward development of the United States.

European immigrants first came to the area around 1833, after Chief Blackhawk, leader of the Potawatomi and Mascouten Indians, signed a treaty with the U.S. government agreeing to relocate his tribes to the other side of the Mississippi River.

One of the earliest settlers to the area was Captain Daniel Wright in 1834, who lived in what is now Half Day, in Lake County. The village was then known as Halfda, after a friendly Indian chief, but due to some bureaucratic misunderstandings, was later recorded as Half Day.

Other prominent settlers include Peter Shaddle (Mundelein area, 1835), George Vardin and Hiram Kennicott (Libertyville area, 1834), Trumball Kent and Johann Sunderlage (Schaumburg area, 1835), Asa Dunton (Arlington Heights area, 1836), George Ela (Lake Zurich area, 1835), and Justice Bangs and Elisha Hubbard (Wauconda area, 1834). Of course, there are countless other families whose significance to the development of the suburbs is forever enshrined in the names of streets and parks.

While these villages did prosper and grow, it wasn't until the 1950s that the true suburban population boom began. Developers began to build affordable housing in villages like Streamwood, Schaumburg, and Arlington Heights for veterans returning from the Korean War. Urban sprawl had begun.

Though somewhat exceptional, the history of Schaumburg reflects much of what happened in northeastern Illinois over the past 40 years or so. Beginning as a community of less than 200 people, its population reached almost 20,000 by 1970. That growth, along with a handful of incentives, brought large corporations like Motorola and Woodfield Mall, which in turn continued to fuel the population. Today, there are almost 75,000 residents in the village.

As major corporations and businesses have made the suburbs their homes, smaller businesses—retail operations, restaurants, and nightclubs, for instance—have responded to the ever-growing affluence of their clientele. With wealthier patrons, local arts organizations have flourished. Illinois tourism brochures have even expanded to include attractions ranging from Six Flags Great America to the historic Civil War reenactments in the Lake County forest preserves.

Even with all of the growth, contemporary residents have made great efforts to keep in mind one of the very things that drew people to the suburbs in the first place: a healthy, protected environment. As recently as April 1999, Lake County residents approved a multi-million dollar referendum for the purchase of more open space, to be set aside strictly for environmental and passive recreational purposes.

The suburbs as a whole have also taken on a new look in terms of ethnic make-up. While still primarily comprised of a middle-class white population; Asian, Hispanic, and African-American families and business people have instilled the wonderful depth of diversity.

School districts have benefited from the prosperity as well, with area schools consistently ranking higher than state averages in terms of test scores, graduation rates, and per-pupil spending.

The most appealing and successful of the suburban villages are those that have carved a niche in the Chicagoland marketplace.

The conference and convention centers of Rosemont, for instance; the historic and environmental appeal of Barrington and Long Grove; and the shopping malls of Schaumburg all serve as focal points in one way or another for consumers and visitors.

Other villages are in the process of recreating or even discovering such niches, as seen by the substantial downtown redevelopment projects in Arlington Heights and Des Plaines.

Regardless of what point they are at along the path of growth, each of Chicago's Northwest Suburbs has a depth and character all its own and promises the adventure of discovery whether you're a first-time visitor or a lifetime resident.

The Palwaukee Airport in Wheeling.

GETTING AROUND

What's In A Name?

While finding your way around is usually easy, newcomers to the suburbs surrounding Chicago are sometimes confused by the seeming plethora of names for area roadways. Depending on where you find yourself, for instance, locals will variously refer to Lake-Cook Road as Main Street or County Line Road. A quick reference is provided for your peace of mind.

Usually Called	Alternate Name
Dundee Road	Route 68
Golf Road	Route 58
Lake-Cook Road	County Line Road, Main Street (in Barrington only)
Milwaukee Avenue	Milwaukee Road, Route 21, Route 21/45
Northwest Tollway	I-90
Northwest Highway	Route 14
Palatine Highway	Palatine Road, Willow Road (east of Arlington Heights)
Rand Road	Route 12
Route 83	Elmhurst Road, Route 83/45
Route 22	Half Day Road
Route 59	Hough Street (Barrington only)

Otherwise, transportation to Chicago's Northwest Suburbs is a breeze, in no small part due to the fact that the Metra/Union Pacific Northwest train line stops in almost all of the villages along Northwest Highway. Schaumburg can be reached via the Metra/Milwaukee District west line, and Metra/Milwaukee District north line stations in Lake Forest, Libertyville, and Grayslake serve the towns covered in the *North by Northwest* section.

By Train

Metra Passenger Services
Weekdays (8 a.m. - 5 p.m.), 312/322-6777
Evenings and weekends, 312/836-7000

Station Locations and Phone Numbers

Arlington Heights
19 E. Northwest Hwy.
847/253-6365

Arlington Park (race track station)
2121 W. Northwest Hwy.
847/398-4844

Barrington
201 Spring St.
847/381-0065

Cumberland (west Des Plaines)
475 N. Northwest Hwy.
No ticket agent.

Des Plaines
1501 Miner St.
847/824-5920

Lake Forest
10205 N. Waukegan Rd.
No ticket agent at station.

Libertyville
200 W. Lake St. (at Milwaukee Ave.)
847/362-2044

Mount Prospect
13 E. Northwest Hwy.
847/253-5839

Palatine
225 W. Colfax St.
847/359-0043

Schaumburg
2000 S. Springinsguth Rd.
847/895-9260

Grayslake, Lake St., and St. Paul St.
No ticket agent at stations.

Bus Companies

CTA/RTA
312/836-7000

PACE Suburban Bus Company
847/364-8130

By Air

O'Hare International Airport
773/686-2200

Major Airlines at O'Hare

Aer Lingus
800/223-6537

Aeroflot 312/819-2350	**Japan Airlines** 800/525-3663
Air Canada 800/776-3000	**KLM Royal Dutch Airlines** 800/374-7747
Air France 800/237-2747	**Korean Airlines** 800/438-5000
Air India 800/223-7778	**LOT Polish Airlines** 800/223-0593
Air Jamaica 800/523-5585	**Lufthansa** 800/645-3880
Alitalia Airlines 800/223-5730	**Mexicana Airlines** 800/531-7921
America West Airlines 800/433-7300	**Northwest Airlines** 800/531-7921
American Airlines 800/433-7300	**Reno Air** 800/736-6247
American Eagle 800/433-7300	**Scandinavian Airlines** 800/221-2350
British Airways 800/247-9297	**Swissair** 800/221-4750
China Eastern Airlines 312/329-0100	**United Airlines** 800/241-6522
Continental Airlines 800/525-0280	**USAir** 800/428-4322
Delta Airlines 800/221-1212	**TWA** 800/221-2000
El Al Israel 800/223-6700	

TOWNSHIPS

So What the Heck Is a Township, Anyway?

The state of Illinois is divided into counties, and its counties are divided into townships. Some towns, the Barrington area and villages that straddle both Lake and Cook counties, for instance, are in more than one township, but the services offered are the same.

Townships do levy taxes for services like road maintenance, welfare assistance, health programs, and property assessments. It's your township assessor you'll want to visit to complain when you get your property tax bill, although the time to complain is long before you get your tax bill.

Lake County Townships*

Cuba Township
28000 W. Cuba Rd.
Barrington   847/381-1924

Ela Township
95 E. Main St.
Lake Zurich   847/438-7823

Libertyville Township
359 Merrill Ct.
Libertyville   847/816-6800

Vernon Township
3050 N. Main St.
Prairie View   847/634-4600

Wauconda Township
505 Bonner Rd.
Wauconda   847/526-2631

Cook County Townships*

Barrington Township
602 S. Hough St.
Barrington   847/381-5632

Elk Grove Township
2400 S. Arlington Heights Rd.
Elk Grove Village   847/437-0300

Hanover Township
8N180 Rt. 59
Bartlett   630/837-0301

Maine Township
1700 Ballard Rd.
Park Ridge   847/297-2510

Palatine Township
721 S. Quentin Rd.
Palatine   847/358-6700

Schaumburg Township
25 Illinois Blvd.
Hoffman Estates   847/884-0030

Wheeling Township
1616 N. Arlington Heights Rd.
Arlington Heights   847/259-7730

** Includes only those townships serving the Northwest Suburban
communities covered in this guide.*

POPULATIONS

Populations* of Northwest Suburban communities at a glance:

Arlington Heights	76,740
Barrington Total	29,487
Barrington	9,885
Barrington Hills	4,456
Lake Barrington	4,440
North Barrington	2,547
South Barrington	3,630
Deer Park	3,194
Tower Lakes	1,335
Buffalo Grove	41,169
Des Plaines	54,836
Elk Grove Village	34,470
Hawthorn Woods	5,498
Hoffman Estates	48,708
Inverness	6,739
Island Lake	7,464
Kildeer	2,821
Lake Zurich	16,786
Libertyville	19,772
Lincolnshire	5,914
Long Grove	6,058
Mount Prospect	54,040
Mundelein	28,012**
Palatine	44,460
Prospect Heights	15,280
Riverwoods	3,516
Rolling Meadows	22,560
Rosemont	3,954
Schaumburg	74,294
Streamwood	34,258
Vernon Hills	17,792
Wauconda	8,461
Wheeling	30,216

*Source: Northeastern Illinois Planning Commission. Statistics based on 1996 projections unless otherwise noted.

** 1997 Special Census Figure.

THE NORTHWEST TERRITORIES

ARLINGTON
HEIGHTS

The Arlington Heights Memorial Library.

A fountain in downtown Arlington Heights.

ARLINGTON HEIGHTS

Arlington Heights at a Glance

Incorporated: 1887
Population: 76,740
Median Household Income: $74,800
Median Home Value: $236,174

Arlington Heights is among the largest of the Northwest Suburbs, stretching roughly from Lake-Cook Road on the north to I-90 at its southernmost end. Covering such a large geographic area, and considering the population is more than 75,000, it is little wonder that Township High School District 214 is among the largest in the state.

District 214 is also one of the best school districts in the state, a fact you'll find true in almost all of the towns covered in this guide. Students inevitably score high on standardized tests, and a high percentage go on to study at four-year institutions.

Statistics like that draw even more families to area villages. Most single-family detached homes in Arlington Heights have at least a child or two running around in the yard or taking the car out for their first spin.

Town-home and condo prices start around $150,000, and it would be difficult to find many detached houses selling for under $200,000.

To drive through Arlington Heights today is to experience downtown redevelopment first-hand. Construction is taking place everywhere, but no place more apparent than the area south of Northwest Highway, east of Arlington Heights Road.

Assuming construction schedules remain on target, the new millennium will ring in a new look for the village. The development will include a number of condominiums and new businesses, but perhaps most impressive is the effort by village leaders to bring high-quality arts and entertainment to town.

Included in the plans are another suburban home for the famed Chicago improvisational comedy theater Second City, a new home for the much-respected Apple Tree Theater of Highland Park, and a movie theater.

ESSENTIAL CONTACTS

Basics

Arlington Heights Village Hall
33 S. Arlington Heights Rd.   847/368-5000

Arlington Heights Chamber of Commerce
180 N. Arlington Heights Rd.   847/253-1703

Police Department (non-emergency)
33 S. Arlington Heights Rd.   847/577-5622

Fire Department
33 S. Arlington Heights Rd. (non-emergency)   847/577-5645

Police, Fire, and Ambulance (emergency)   911

Townships

Elk Grove Township
2400 S. Arlington Heights Rd.
Elk Grove Village   847/437-0300

Wheeling Township
1616 N. Arlington Heights Rd.
Arlington Heights   847/259-7730

Parks and Recreation

Arlington Heights Park District
410 N. Arlington Heights Rd.   847/577-3000

Libraries

Arlington Heights Memorial Library
500 N. Dunton Ave.   847/392-1119

Schools

School Districts

Arlington Heights School District 25
1200 S. Dunton Ave.   847/758-4870

Community Consolidated School District 21
Kenneth Gill Administrative Center
999 W. Dundee Rd.
Wheeling   847/537-8270

Community Consolidated School District 59
Elk Grove Township Schools
2123 S. Arlington Heights Rd.   847/593-4300

Township High School District 214
Forest View Educational Center
2121 S. Goebbert Rd.   847/718-7600

Community Colleges

Harper College
1200 W. Algonquin Rd.
Palatine   847/925-6000

Roosevelt University
Albert A. Robin Campus
1400 N. Roosevelt Blvd.
Schaumburg   847/619-8600

Houses of Worship

Arlington Assembly of God
116 W. Eastman St.   847/818-1131

Arlington Countryside Church
916 E. Hintz Rd.   847/255-2140

Arlington Heights Evangelical Free Church
1331 N. Belmont Ave.   847/392-4840

Chinese Baptist Church of the Northwest Suburbs
(Southern Baptist Convention)
1640 S. Arlington Heights Rd.   847/228-6066

Christian Church of Arlington Heights
333 W. Thomas Ave.   847/259-0059

Church of Christian Liberty and Academy
502 W. Euclid Ave.   847/259-8736

Church of the Incarnation
330 Golf Rd.   847/956-1510

Church of Jesus Christ of Latter Day Saints
2035 N. Windsor Dr.   847/398-9662

Congregational United Church of Christ
1001 W. Kirchoff Rd.   847/392-6650

Cross and Crown Community Church
1122 W. Rand Rd.   847/394-0362

Crossroads Community Church
116 S. Arlington Heights Rd.   847/506-1511

Faith Lutheran Church (Missouri Synod)
421 S. Arlington Heights Rd.   847/253-4839

First Baptist Church of Arlington Heights
1211 W. Campbell Ave.   847/392-1712

First Church of Christ Scientist
401 S. Evergreen Ave.   847/253-3366

First Presbyterian Church of Arlington Heights
302 N. Dunton Ave.   847/255-5900

First United Methodist Church of Arlington Heights
1903 E. Euclid Ave.   847/255-5112

Living Christ Lutheran Church (Missouri Synod)
625 E. Dundee Rd.   847/577-7133

Lutheran Church of the Cross (Lutheran Church in America)
2025 S. Goebbert Rd.   847/437-5141

Messiah Lutheran Church (Missouri Synod)
1323 N. Ridge Ave.   847/253-9881

Our Lady of the Wayside Roman Catholic Church
432 W. Park Ave.   847/253-5353

Our Savior's Lutheran Church (Lutheran Church in America)
1234 N. Arlington Heights Rd.   847/255-8700

St. Edna Catholic Church
2525 N. Arlington Heights Rd.   847/398-3362

St. James Catholic Church
820 N. Arlington Heights Rd.   847/253-6305

St. John United Church of Christ
308 S. Evergreen Ave.   847/255-6687

St. Peter Lutheran Church (Missouri Synod)
111 W. Olive St.   847/259-4114

St. Simon's Episcopal Church
717 Kirchoff Rd.   847/259-2930

Southminster Presbyterian Church
916 E. Central Rd.   847/392-1060

True Jesus Church
111 W. Henry St.   847/259-8014

Beth Tikvah Congregation
300 Hillcrest Blvd.
Hoffman Estates   847/885-4545

Congregation B'nai Maccabim
1731 Deerfield Rd.
Highland Park   847/432-8580

Congregation B'nai Shalom
701 W. Aptakisic Rd.
Buffalo Grove   847/541-1460

Conservative United Synagogue of America
Congregation Beth Judea
Rt. 83 and Hilltop Rd.
Long Grove   847/634-0777

Temple Chai
1670 Checker Rd.
Long Grove   847/537-1771

DINING

Native's Choices

La Tasca Tapas Restaurant
25 W. Davis St.
847/398-2400
If you aren't familiar with tapas-style dining, or even if you are, for
that matter, you're in for a real treat at La Tasca. The atmosphere is

lively and fun, but retains that European sense of anonymity for those looking for a romantic evening. Tapas plates generally range from about $3.95 to $6.95, but be careful as they can add up if you aren't paying attention. A plate of wonderful marinated olives and bread is set on the table as soon as you're seated. Order their excellent homemade red or white sangria to wash them down.
Open Mon. - Sat. 11 a.m. - 11 p.m., Sun. 4 p.m. - 11 p.m.

Le Titi de Paris
1015 W. Dundee Rd.
847/506-0222
If you appreciate fine dining, marvelous presentation, and elegant French cuisine, you cannot miss this gem of a restaurant. Chef and owner Pierre Pollin's long and distinguished background shows with every selection, from the appetizer of Caspian beluga caviar to the nut-crusted loin of veal. The wine list features literally hundreds of selections with something in every price range; don't hesitate to ask for a suggestion. Expect to spend in the neighborhood of $40 to $50 per person, not including cocktails or wine.
Open for lunch Tues. - Fri. 11:30 a.m.; for dinner Tues. - Fri. 5:30 p.m., Sat. 5 p.m. Closed Sun. - Mon.

Jameson's Char House
1331 W. Dundee Rd.
847/392-7100
Jameson's ranks among my favorite suburban restaurants for the money, in part because the cuts of meat and fish are impeccably fresh, but also because they treat you like a regular the moment you walk through the door. The large, horseshoe-shaped bar is a popular after-work meeting place for locals.
Open Mon. - Sat. 11 a.m. - 10 p.m., Sun. 12 p.m. - 10 p.m.

Regina's Ristorante
27 W. Campbell St.
847/394-2728
Phil and Regina Campinella have created the true feeling of Italian dining in their small, intimate restaurant, right down to the homegrown herbs used in the kitchen. The appetizer of mussels in marinara sauce is spicier than most, but addictive, and the *zuppa di pesce* is swimming with seafood. Dinner entrees range from $9.95 to $19.95.
Open for dinner 4:30 p.m. daily. Closed Mon.

Worth Noting

Ada's Famous Deli & Restaurant
902 W. Dundee Rd.
847/577-7444
This wonderful kosher-style deli features a large dining room with pickles at every table. Once, fighting a cold, I ordered the matzo ball soup, and I swear to this day that the cold disappeared because of it. The corned beef sandwich on rye is incredible, and portions are enormous. Prices are very reasonable, between $4.95 and $10.95.
Open Sun. - Thurs. 7 a.m. - 10 p.m., Fri. - Sat. 7 a.m. - 12 a.m.

Arlington Grill
2 E. Northwest Hwy.
847/577-9292
Another popular breakfast and lunch diner with "fresh ham on the bone daily."
Open daily 6 a.m. - 3 p.m.

Arlington Trackside
2000 W. Euclid Ave.
847/259-8400
The food at this off-track betting facility isn't as good as it should be, frankly, but most people don't care since they're there for the horses. Besides, this is the only place in the suburbs where you have the chance to leave with more money than you brought.
Open daily 11 a.m. - the last race or midnight.

Bill's Inn
20 W. Northwest Hwy.
847/255-5835
It's dark and often smoky, but Bill's is one of my favorite dive bars anywhere. Maybe because they serve Guinness Stout at the right temperature, or maybe because of the erudite bartender, Wally. Don't even think about food.
Open Mon. - Thurs. 8 a.m. - 12 a.m., Fri. - Sat. 8 a.m. - 1 a.m.

Delaney & Murphy Steak House
3400 W. Euclid Ave.
847/394-2000
In the Arlington Park Hilton, this friendly, relaxed spot features great

steaks and a variety of American cuisine (about $10-$25, most items below $16). Live music in the piano bar Tuesday through Saturday. *Open Mon. - Sat. 5:30 p.m. - 10 p.m.*

Dunton House
11 W. Davis St.
847/394-5885
A basic American breakfast-and-lunch diner. Everything is decent, prices are low, and service is friendly.
Open daily 5 a.m. - aprox. 10 p.m.

Eddie's Restaurant and Lounge
10 E. Northwest Hwy.
847/253-1320
Your basic traditional American fare served without pretense or fuss. The Friday fish fry draws a crowd. Prices generally $5.95-$12.95.
Open Mon. - Sat. 11 a.m. - 11 p.m., Sun. 4 p.m. - 11 p.m.

Granny's
24 E. Miner St.
847/398-1720
A family-style diner, but this one is open for dinner. Prices are low, and the menu has that inexplicably odd mix of things from Greek salads to vegetable stir-fries. Prices for full meals start around $5.
Open Tues. - Sat. 6 a.m. - 10 p.m., Sun. - Mon. 6 a.m. - 9 p.m.

Harry's of Arlington
1 N. Vail Ave.
847/577-2525
One of the top contenders for best suburban "neighborhood pub" features a better-than-average bar menu, friendly crowds, occasional live music on weekends, and a decent selection of beers. Casual. Meals from about $6.95 to $11.95.
Open Mon. - Thurs. 11 a.m. - 1 a.m., Fri. - Sat. 11 a.m. - 2 a.m., Sun. 11 a.m. - 12 a.m.

Jimmy's Place
640 W. Northwest Hwy.
847/398-9783
Another popular hangout among locals, noted for cold beers and cheap eats. They boast about their barbecued ribs for good reason, and the pizza is always a good bet. Prices range from about $5.95 to

$10.95.
Open daily 10:30 a.m. - 10 p.m.

La Chicanita Mexican Restaurant
202 N. Dunton Ave.
847/255-7075
When I'm asked for a good Mexican restaurant in the suburbs, this is the first place that comes to mind. Be sure to try the homemade tamales when they're available, and the fajitas are outstanding. Wash it all down with a great margarita. Entrees from about $5.95 to $15.
Open Mon. - Thurs. 10 a.m. - 10 p.m., Fri. - Sat. 10 a.m. - 11 p.m., Sun. 10 a.m. - 9 p.m.

Rapp's
602 W. Northwest Hwy.
847/253-3544
Rapp's has been around forever, sort of a staple among the over-50 crowd. Don't be shy if you're younger than that; the food is consistently good, and you'll probably make a new friend. Meals $7.95-$15.
Open Sun. - Thurs. 11 a.m. - 10 p.m., Fri. - Sat. 11 a.m. - 11 p.m.

Rokbonki Japanese Steak House
876 W. Dundee Rd.
847/506-1212
The blinding swirl of knives, the clack of shakers full of seasonings, and the sizzle of fish and vegetables on a flat grill all combine for a marvelous presentation. Prices start around $15 per plate; you're paying mostly for the show.
Open Mon. - Thurs. 5 p.m. - 10 p.m., Fri. - Sat. 5 p.m. - 11 p.m., Sun. 4:30 p.m. - 10 p.m.

Vail Street Café
19 N. Vail Ave.
847/392-1164
The Vail Street is a gem, not so much because of the large bagels and variety of coffees, which are all good, but because of the owners' support of the local art scene. Original art fills the walls on a rotating basis; weekends feature live music and poetry readings; and they've recently ventured into theater presentations. The café is a cultural favorite and is likely to be even more popular as the downtown Arlington Heights renovations are completed.
Open daily 6 a.m. - 3 p.m. Call for evening performance hours.

La Zingara Trattoria
2300 E. Rand Rd.
847/398-3700
The newest entry into the local restaurant scene is a wonderful little brightly colored haven with authentic Italian cuisine. I like the Pennette Za' Za' and the Ravioli Campagnola, in particular. Prices range from $9.95 to $18.95.
Open for lunch Tues. - Fri. 11 a.m. - 2:30 p.m.; for dinner Tues. - Thurs. 2:30 p.m. - 10:30 p.m., Fri. - Sat. 2:30 p.m. - 11:30 p.m., Sun. 3 p.m. - 10 p.m. Closed Mon.

THE BARRINGTONS

Barrington, Barrington Hills, South Barrington, North Barrington, Deer Park, Inverness, Lake Barrington, and Tower Lakes

The Octagon House in Barrington.

Barrington and Inverness

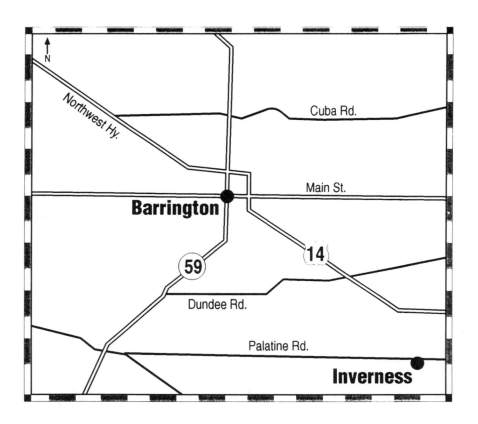

THE BARRINGTONS

Barrington at a Glance

Incorporated: 1865
Population: 9,875
Median Household Income: $99,200
Median Home Value: $307,000

The history of the combined Barrington communities is notable for its marked care in development. Today, Northwest Highway (Route 14) is the backbone of retail development, but the quaint downtown business district has been aggressively preserved.

The village of Barrington and its nearby "suburbs" are North Shore communities without the shore, although several small lakes, ponds, and marshes dot the landscape. Each village has its own government, but the Barrington Area Council of Governments serves as a shared vehicle through which the major developmental and business interests of the communities are defended.

An organization called Citizens for Conservation plays a critical role in preserving the local natural environment and open spaces. That process sometimes leads to the perception by outsiders of a "Not In My Back Yard," or NIMBY, attitude.

If that attitude is the worst thing about the Barringtons, it's also the best thing. Ideally, the villages seek to maintain a high level of education, demanding standards for residential and corporate development and a high quality of life for area residents while preserving the delicate environmental resources native to northern Illinois.

The populations of the various towns include a number of corporate executives, a handful of sports superstars (including former Chicago Bear running back Walter Payton), and a number of horse owners. As proof, consider the beautiful, sprawling estate of Arlington International Racecourse owner Richard Duchossois, which lies just west of the village along Lake-Cook Road (called Main Street in downtown Barrington). During nice weather, this drive will strip away stress with each passing mile.

Barrington Hills at a Glance

Incorporated: 1957
Population: 4,456
Median Household Income: $173,500
Median Home Value: $500,000

South Barrington at a Glance

Incorporated: 1958
Population: 3,630
Median Household Income: $233,000
Median Home Value: $500,000

North Barrington at a Glance

Incorporated: 1959
Population: 2,547
Median Household Income: $204,800
Median Home Value: $463,000

Another sign of the equestrian interests of area residents is the fact that the *minimum* residential lot requirement in Barrington Hills is five acres, and every other yard here is filled with at least one horse.

True, property values and property taxes in the roughly 72-square-mile area are high compared to nearby villages, but Community Unit School District 220, where most property tax dollars are spent, is ranked among the finest in the country. More than 90 percent of the high school graduates here attend some form of higher education.

The average home sells for around $300,000, but visits to Barrington Hills, South Barrington, and North Barrington will reveal homes and estates valued at more than $1 million.

The arts community in Barrington is extremely active. Fine samples of the work of local artists can be seen and purchased at the Barrington Area Arts Council Gallery (207 Park Ave). Community residents serve on boards of organizations, including the Lyric Opera, the Joffrey Ballet of Chicago, the Chicago Symphony Orchestra, and the Art

Institute of Chicago.

The area features a number of restaurants, almost all of which are well worth a visit. There is however, little nightlife in the area other than the historic Catlow Theater, which offers first-rate, second-run films at discounted prices.

While newcomers to the area might be a bit confused by the different village names, most residents are happy enough to call their home "Barrington," no matter what their address is.

Deer Park at a Glance

Incorporated: 1957
Population: 3,194
Median Household Income: $208,250
Median Home Value: $478,000

Inverness at a Glance

Incorporated: 1962
Population: 6,739
Median Household Income: $220,545
Median Home Value: $500,000

Lake Barrington at a Glance

Incorporated: 1959
Population: 4,440
Median Household Income: $149,000
Median Home Value: $374,600

Tower Lakes at a Glance

Incorporated: 1966
Population: 1,335
Median Household Income: $182,000
Median Home Value: $397,000

ESSENTIAL CONTACTS

Basics

Barrington Village Hall
1301 S. Grove Ave., Ste. 200 (interim location) 847/842-5050
206 S. Hough St. (permanent site)

Barrington Hills Village Hall
112 Algonquin Rd.   847/551-3000
Barrington Hills

Deer Park Village Hall
21040 N. Rand Rd.   847/726-1648
Lake Zurich

Inverness Village Hall
1400 Baldwin Rd.   847/358-7740
Inverness

Lake Barrington Village Hall
23860 N. Old Barrington Rd.   847/381-6010
Barrington

North Barrington Village Hall
111 Old Barrington Rd.   847/381-3393
North Barrington

South Barrington Village Hall
30 S. Barrington Rd.   847/381-7510
South Barrington

Tower Lakes Village Hall
400 N. Rt. 59   847/526-0488

Barrington Area Council of Governments (BACOG)
800 S. Northwest Hwy.   847/381-7871

Barrington Area Chamber of Commerce
325 N. Hough St.   847/381-2525

Police Department (non-emergency)
121 W. Station St.   847/381-2141

Fire Department (non-emergency)
121 W. Station St.   847/381-2141

Paramedics (non-emergency)   847/381-2141

Police, Fire, and Ambulance (emergency)   911

Townships

Barrington Township
602 S. Hough St.   847/381-5632

Cuba Township
28000 W. Cuba Rd.   847/381-1924

Ela Township
95 E. Main St.
Lake Zurich   847/438-7823

Palatine Township
721 S. Quentin Rd.
Palatine   847/358-6700

Parks and Recreation

Barrington Countryside Park District
Barrington Hills   847/381-1911

Barrington Park District
Langendorf Park
235 Lions Dr.   847/381-0687

Inverness Park District
1400 Baldwin Rd.   847/776-9411

Lake Barrington Park District
23860 N. Old Barrington Rd.   847/381-6010

South Barrington Park District
3 Tennis Club Dr.   847/381-7515

Libraries

Barrington Area Library
505 N. Northwest Hwy.   847/382-1300

Schools

School Districts

Community Unit School District 220
310 E. James St.   847/381-6300

Community Colleges

Harper College
1200 W. Algonquin Rd.
Palatine   847/925-6000

Roosevelt University
Albert A. Robin campus
1400 N. Roosevelt Blvd.
Schaumburg   847/619-8600

Selected Community Organizations

Barrington Area Arts Council and Gallery
207 Park Ave.   847/382-5626

Barrington Area Council on Aging
301 E. Main St.   847/382-5030

Barrington Area Development Council   847/382-4357

Barrington Area Historical Society
218 W. Main St.   847/381-1730

Barrington Education Association
Barrington High School
616 W. Main St.   847/381-1400

Barrington Junior Women's Club   847/622-3838

Barrington Police Benevolent Association   847/381-2141

Barrington Women's Club
181-B Club Cir.
Lake Barrington   847/381-9288

Citizens for Conservation
211 N. Ela Rd.   847/382-7283

League of Women Voters   847/382-3288

Newcomers Club of Barrington   847/842-1000

Volunteer Center of Greater Barrington   847/842-9930

Houses of Worship

Barrington United Methodist Church
311 S. Hough St.   847/381-1725

Community Church of Barrington
407 S. Grove Ave.   847/381-1294

First Church of Christian Scientist
421 E. Main St.   847/381-0408

Holy Family Catholic Church
2515 Palatine Rd.
Inverness   847/359-0042

Lutheran Church of the Atonement
909 E. Main St.   847/381-0243

New Friends Wesleyan Church
Rt. 68 and Sutton Rd.
Barrington Hills   847/551-9212

Presbyterian Church of Barrington
6 Brinker Rd.   847/381-0975

St. Anne Catholic Church
Franklin and Ela streets   847/382-5300

St. Mark's Episcopal Church
337 Ridge Rd.   847/381-0596

St. Matthew Lutheran Church
720 Dundee Ave.   847/382-7002

St. Michael's Episcopal Church
647 Dundee Ave.   847/381-2323

St. Paul United Church of Christ
401 E. Main St.   847/381-0460

Salem United Methodist Church
115 W. Lincoln Ave.   847/381-0524

Village Church of Barrington
1600 E. Main St.   847/381-5221

Willow Creek Community Church
67 E. Algonquin Rd.
South Barrington   847/765-5000

Beth Tikvah Congregation (Reform)
300 Hillcrest Ave.
Hoffman Estates   847/885-4545

Congregation Kneseth Israel (Conservative)
330 Division St.
Elgin   847/741-5656

DINING

Native's Choices

Ambrosia Euro-American Patisserie
710 W. Northwest Hwy.
847/304-8278
You will not find a better gourmet bakery and pastry shop anywhere. The creations are unique, mouthwatering, and generally decadent, earning the chef/owners a spot on the PBS *Great Chefs* series.
Open Tues. - Fri. 7 a.m. - 6 p.m., Sat. 7 a.m. - 4 p.m., Sun. 7 a.m. - 1 p.m. Closed Mon.

The Canteen
214 S. Hough St.
847/381-9844
I'll call this a greasy spoon, but with all the affection I can muster. The venerable Canteen has probably been the source of more stories, and more discussions about stories, than any place on the Barrington beat. Each morning, against a backdrop of sizzling bacon and the smell of piping hot coffee, long-time locals and a handful of politicians pour over newspapers and hash out the news of the day.
Open Mon. - Sat. 5 a.m. - 3 p.m. Closed Sun.

Chessie's Restaurant
Ice House Mall
200 Applebee St.
847/382-5020
This is where almost all the locals go for lunch, be it business or pleasure. The menu is varied, with an emphasis on healthy salads, sandwiches, and pastas ($7.95-$15.95). Service is excellent.
Open Mon. - Thurs. 11:30 a.m. - 10 p.m., Fri. 11:30 a.m. - 11 p.m., Sat. 11 a.m. - 11 p.m., Sun. 10 a.m. - 9 p.m.

Frantonio's Deli and Café
421 N. Northwest Hwy.
847/382-2997
One of the most authentic Italian delis in the suburbs. In addition to a large variety of hot and cold sandwiches and salads, Frantonio's offers homemade mozzarella and a number of Italian grocery specialties.

Most items are well under $10. I love this place! *Open Mon. 9 a.m. - 3 p.m., Tues. - Fri. 9 a.m. - 6:30 p.m., Sat. 9 a.m. - 5 p.m. Closed Sun.*

The Greenery Restaurant
117 North Ave.
847/381-9000
Young chef J. Andrew Coates has quickly made a name for himself in this quaint Victorian house-*cum*-restaurant. The menu features an array of very creative and eclectic American cuisine along with an award-winning wine selection. Expect to spend at least $30 to $40 per person. *Open daily 5:30 p.m. - aprox. 9 p.m., Fri. - Sat. until 10 p.m.*

The Millrose Brewing Co.
45 S. Barrington Rd.
South Barrington
847/382-7673
Bill Rose is among the several founding fathers of the village of South Barrington, where his meat packing company, the Rose Packing Co., is based. The restaurant and microbrewery adjacent to the corporation is exceptional, both in design and food, and prices reflect that. The interior of the bar resembles a large mountain lodge; the restaurant would be the envy of any country club. Food is excellent, with red meat the recommended choice. The selection of microbrews here outclasses Chicago's Goose Island Brewery by a long shot. *Open for lunch Mon. - Sat. 11 a.m. - 3:30 p.m.; for dinner Mon. - Thurs. 3:30 p.m. - 10 p.m., Fri. - Sat. 3:30 p.m. - 11 p.m., Sun. 12 p.m. - 9 p.m.*

Sagano Japanese Restaurant
110 N. Hough St.
847/382-8980
Sagano is one of the only authentic sushi and sashimi bars in the suburbs. More importantly, it's the absolute best. The quality and freshness of the seafood preparations are impeccable, but if you just can't swallow a slice of raw tuna, there is an extensive menu of traditional cooked Japanese dishes. Prices at both lunch and dinner are quite reasonable at $6.95 to $15; some of the more exotic sashimi dishes can run much higher. *Open for lunch Mon. - Fri. 11:30 a.m. - 2:30 p.m.; for dinner Mon. - Thurs. 5 p.m. - 9:45 p.m., Fri. - Sat. 5 p.m. - 10:30 p.m., Sun. 4 p.m. - 9 p.m.*

Worth Noting

Barn of Barrington
1415 S. Barrington Rd.
847/381-8585
This is the place for a wedding or banquet, but if you're still looking for the perfect match, it's also a popular meeting place for a couple of Northwest Suburban singles groups. The food is very good and service is commendable, though the atmosphere is a bit, well, banquetish. Prices range from $10.95 to $22.
Open for lunch Tues. - Fri. 11:30 a.m. - 2:30 p.m.; for dinner Tues. - Thurs. 5 p.m. - 9 p.m., Fri. - Sat. 5 p.m. -10 p.m.; for brunch Sun. 10:30 a.m. - 2 p.m.

Barrington Country Bistro
700 W. Northwest Hwy.
847/842-1300
The restaurant is billed as a French country bistro, but it's in pretty nice country. Dress is at the nicer end of casual; prices are at the higher end of moderate. Both food and wine selections are excellent, as is the service. Expect to spend around $30 per person.
Open for lunch Mon. - Sat. 11:30 a.m. - 2 p.m.; for dinner Sun. - Thurs. 5 p.m. - 8:30 p.m., Fri. - Sat. 5 p.m. - 9:30 p.m.

Boloney's Sandwich Shop
114 W. Main St.
847/381-0645
Great sandwiches and fantastic soups are the order of the day at this favorite lunch and snack shop located in the Catlow movie theater building. Here, two people can actually have a meal *and* catch a great second-run flick for less than $20.
Open Mon. - Sat. 10 a.m. - 9 p.m.

Kelsey Road House
352 Kelsey Rd.
847/381-8300
Although a little off the beaten path (you'll travel north on Northwest Highway for a mile or two before reaching Kelsey Road), the Kelsey Road House is well worth the visit. In summer months they open the outdoor patio; get there early to find a table. The fare is strictly road-house—sandwiches and burgers for the most part, but all items are

well-prepared. The interior is dark, intimate, and brimming with character. Prices are very reasonable: around $5.95 to $12.95. *Open Sun. - Thurs. 11:30 a.m. - 10 p.m., Fri. - Sat. 11:30 a.m. - 11 p.m.*

The Market House
110 E. Lake St.
847/382-4782
One of Barrington's newer dining establishments, The Market House is among the only area restaurants to specialize in seafood. Excellent cuts of beef, pork, and game are also available. The atmosphere is intimate and home-spun.
Open Mon. - Thurs. 5 p.m. - 9 p.m., Fri. - Sat. 5 p.m. - 10 p.m. Closed Sun.

Penny Road Pub
164 Old Sutton Rd.
847/428-0562
Ask a local for directions to this friendly little out-of-the way neighborhood bar with a hard-rock jukebox and attitude to match. On weekends you'll often find live music, but more often you'll just find good company and a surprising menu that boasts almost a dozen different burgers. Nothing on the menu is more than $10.
Open Mon. - Sat. 10:30 a.m. - 4 a.m. Closed Sun.

RSVP's
333 W. Northwest Hwy.
847/381-5530
Once upon a time, this was a bar attached to a bowling alley. Now the alley is gone, but the bar and a small kitchen survive. In my early reporter and editor days, this was where I went to wind down and talk stories with the locals. Lunch prices are generally well under $10.
Open Mon. - Thurs. 10 a.m. - 12 a.m., Fri. - Sat. 10 a.m. - 2 a.m. Closing hours may vary depending on crowd. Closed Sun.

Wildflower Continental Bistro
222 S. Cook St.
847/277-0964
Opened in Dec. 1998, the Wildflower still has a way to go to prove its staying power. Strong indicators of its success include a wonderfully colorful interior design and a menu that seems to fit perfectly with the target clientele. Meals are prepared simply and without a lot of frills,

ingredients are fresh, and flavors are easy on the palate. No alcohol is served, which helps keep prices very affordable.
Open for lunch Mon. 11 a.m. - 3:30 p.m., Tues. - Sat. 11 a.m. - 3:30 p.m.; for dinner Tues. - Thurs. 5 p.m. - 8:30 p.m., Fri. - Sat. 5 p.m. - 9:30 p.m. Closed Sun.

Yankee Doodle Inn
Behind Village Liquors on Main St.
847/381-1098
Like RSVP's (see p. 46), this friendly bar seems a little out of place in a town like Barrington. The interior is dim and generally smoky, but the inexpensive drinks and friendly atmosphere, along with its convenient proximity to the Barrington train station, continue to draw a "regulars" kind of crowd.
Open Mon. - Sat. 9 a.m. - 1 a.m., Sun. 11 a.m. - 9:30 p.m.

BUFFALO GROVE, WHEELING, LONG GROVE, AND PROSPECT HEIGHTS

The sign for Long Grove's popular Confectionery Co.

Long Grove, Buffalo Grove, and Wheeling

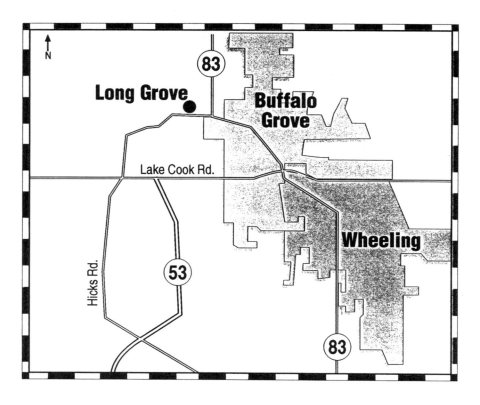

BUFFALO GROVE

Buffalo Grove at a Glance

Incorporated: 1958
Population: 41,169
Median Household Income: $88,335
Median Home Value: $235,400

Before the earliest settlers moved into the area to build lumber mills, office buildings, and Dairy Queens, the suburbs were simple, unspoiled lands. The geography was mostly flat, but was dotted with groves made up of native-grass prairies and wooded lands.

Elk Grove Village and Buffalo Grove still bear the names that reflect this early environment, though few reminders are left of that heritage.

Buffalo Grove is far more than a bedroom community, with significant retail and office developments on its south border and in the Town Center strip mall at McHenry and Lake-Cook roads. Still, until relatively recently the village struggled to find an anchor tenant for the high-traffic site. It will now be home to a large grocery store, and other tenants are expected to follow.

Overall, Buffalo Grove is a pleasant and quiet town, filled with churches and synagogues and a general sense of family values. Most of the village is made up of single-family homes, filled with the suburban prototype—mom, dad, two or more children, a dog, a couple of televisions, and several phone lines. The median home value is around $235,000, and the median income is $88,000.

The park district boasts two of the best and busiest golf courses in the area, as well as several other recreational opportunities. And while there is not much nightlife in town, Wheeling's Restaurant Row (see p. 63) is just down the street.

ESSENTIAL CONTACTS

Basics

Buffalo Grove Village Hall
50 Raupp Blvd.   847/459-2500

Buffalo Grove Chamber of Commerce
50 Raupp Blvd.   847/541-7799

Police Department (non-emergency)
46 Raupp Blvd.   847/459-2560

Fire Department (non-emergency)
1051 Highland Grove Dr.   847/537-0995

Police, Fire, and Ambulance (emergency)   911

Townships

Vernon Township
2050 N. Main St.   847/634-4600

Wheeling Township
1616 N. Arlington Heights Rd.
Arlington Heights   847/259-7730

Parks and Recreation

Buffalo Grove Park District
Alcott Community Center and Administration offices
530 Bernard Dr.   847/459-5700

Parks Department offices
150 Raupp Blvd.   847/459-2311

Libraries

Indian Trails Public Library
355 S. Schoenbeck Rd.
Wheeling   847/459-4100

Vernon Area Public Library
300 Olde Half Day Rd.
Lincolnshire   847/634-3650

Schools

School Districts

Elementary School District 21
999 W. Dundee Rd.
Wheeling   847/537-8270

Elementary School District 96
777 Checker Dr.
Buffalo Grove   847/459-4260

Elementary School District 102
1231 Weiland Rd.
Buffalo Grove   847/634-1358

Elementary School District 103
1370 Riverwoods Rd.
Lake Forest   847/295-4030

High School District 214
2121 S. Goebbert Rd.
Arlington Heights   847/437-4600

Stevenson High School District 125
1 Stevenson Dr.
Lincolnshire   847/634-4000

Private Elementary Schools

St. Mary's School
50 N. Buffalo Grove Rd.   847/459-6270

Community Colleges

College of Lake County
19351 W. Washington St.
Grayslake   847/233-6601

Harper College
1200 W. Algonquin Rd.
Palatine   847/925-6000

Selected Community Organizations

Buffalo Grove Fine Arts
Buffalo Grove Park District
530 Bernard Dr.   847/459-5700, x.132

Buffalo Grove Historical Society
Buffalo Grove Park District
530 Bernard Dr.   847/459-5700, x.116

Buffalo Grove Senior Citizens
Buffalo Grove Park District
530 Bernard Dr.   847/459-5700

Buffalo Grove Welcome Wagon
3000 Acacia Terr.   847/913-9887

Omni Youth Services
1616 N. Arlington Heights Rd.
Arlington Heights   847/253-6010

Houses of Worship

The Church of Jesus Christ of Latter-Day Saints
15 Port Clinton Rd.   847/913-5414

Hope Lutheran Church
1660 Checker Rd.
Long Grove   847/634-2070

Kingswood United Methodist Church
401 W. Dundee Rd.   847/398-0770

Living Christ Lutheran Church
625 E. Dundee Rd.
Arlington Heights   847/577-7133

New Life Lutheran Church
2600 N. Buffalo Grove Rd.   847/520-9176

Rock of Israel Messianic Congregation
(Jewish-Christian Fellowship)
Arlington Heights Rd. (north of Lake-Cook Rd.) 847/520-0616

St. Mary's Catholic Church
75 N. Buffalo Grove Rd.   847/541-1450

Village Baptist Church
385 N. Buffalo Grove Rd.   847/537-7172

Westminster Christian Fellowship
16670 Easton Ave.
Prairie View   847/634-3333

Congregation Beth Am (Reform)
850 Jenkins Court
Wheeling   847/459-1677

Congregation Beth Judea (Conservative)
Rt. 83 and Hilltop Rd.
Long Grove   847/634-0777

Congregation B'nai Shalom (Traditional)
701 W. Aptakisic Rd.   847/541-1460

Congregation Mishpaha (Reform)
Call for meeting place.   847/459-3279

Congregation Shirat Emet (Reform)
Call for meeting place.   847/541-7273

Lubavitch Chabad (Orthodox)
16296 W. Aptakisic Rd.
Prairie View   847/808-7770

Project Seed of Suburban Chicago (Orthodox)
158 McHenry Rd.   847/215-7664

Temple Chai (Reform)
1670 Checker Rd.
Long Grove   847/537-1771

Temple Shir Shalom (Reform)
325 Lexington Dr.   847/465-0101

DINING

Native's Choices

Cilantro
154 N. McHenry Rd.
847/520-9988
Cantonese take-out places used to be the norm for Chinese food in
the suburbs, but restaurants like Cilantro have thankfully changed
that for good. There is a gourmet touch to almost everything on the
menu, evident in fresh ingredients and light, savory sauces. The focus
is mainly on Szechuan and Mandarin dishes, though you'll also find
a handful of old standbys. Prices range from $8.95 to $16.50.
Open Mon. - Thurs. 11 a.m. - 10 p.m., Fri. - Sat. 11 a.m. - 11 p.m.,
Sun. 11:30 a.m. - 10:30 p.m.

Deerfields of Buffalo Grove
201 N. Buffalo Grove Rd.
847/520-0068
My grandmother used to live just down the street from the original Deerfield's Bakery, so I have a soft spot in my heart for their marvelous pastries. This newer location in Buffalo Grove is just as popular and just as good. You'll be amazed at the lines that form when holidays roll around.
Open Mon. - Sat. 6 a.m. - 6:30 p.m., Sun. 7 a.m. - 1 p.m.

Lou Malnati's Pizzeria
85 S. Buffalo Grove Rd., 847/215-7100
1050 E. Higgins Rd., Elk Grove Village, 847/439-2000
1 S. Roselle Rd., Schaumburg, 847/985-1525
This is a small, local chain that features great deep-dish pizza and heaping plates of Italian fare in a sports club atmosphere. Prices are average, about $8.95 to $16.95, and service is generally good, although crowds get thick at peak times.
Open Mon. - Thurs. 11 a.m. - 11 p.m., Fri. - Sat. 11 a.m. - 12 a.m., Sun. 12 p.m. - 11 p.m.

Worth Noting

Chef Tony's Taste of Spain
86 W. Dundee Rd.
847/520-8222
If you're in the mood for a light lunch or dinner, this is the place. Chef Tony's large selection of tapas and Spanish-inspired dishes (paella and the like) is generally very good, and it's obvious that most locals agree; the place has been around as long as I can remember. Tapas dishes fall around $3.95, entrees between $8.95 and $15.95.
Open daily 11 a.m. - 10 p.m.

Crawdaddy Bayou

Scenes from Crawdaddy Bayou on Wheeling's "Restaurant Row":
Hot sauce and other Cajun specialties for sale in the gift shop (*left*) and
the "gator"—the only one that goes hungry at this favorite
Northwest Suburban eatery (*right*).

WHEELING

Wheeling at a Glance

Incorporated: 1894
Population: 30,216
Median Household Income: $58,800
Median Home Value: $149,958

When it comes to entertainment history, the village of Wheeling has other area communities beat, hands down.

Nowhere else can claim, for instance, to have hosted the legendary trio of Frank Sinatra, Dean Martin, and Sammy Davis Jr. for a week-long series of appearances in a club owned by none other than mob boss Sam Giancana.

A CD released in 1999, "The Summit," celebrates the performances, which took place in Nov. 1962, but sadly, that's all that remains of the date. The nightclub itself, called Villa Venice, burned down in 1967. Older residents and documents at the Wheeling Historical Society relate that the restaurant in its heyday was quite the place to visit, with gondolas trolling the Des Plaines River and lanterns lighting the patio.

Today, people in canoes can occasionally be seen paddling down the river, but otherwise the only recreational entertainment it provides is scenic.

Wheeling is a demographically diverse community, with Hispanic and Asian residents making up around 9 percent (combined) of the total population.

Local leaders have long struggled with the general appearance and business health of the downtown district along Dundee Road and Milwaukee Avenue, but they hit the jackpot with the development and cultivation of "Restaurant Row" (see p. 63). As of the printing of this guide, at least one more restaurant was expected to open by fall of 1999.

ESSENTIAL CONTACTS

Basics

Municipal Center
255 W. Dundee Rd.   847/459-2600

Wheeling/Prospect Heights Area Chamber of Commerce
395 E. Dundee Rd.   847/541-0170

Police Department (non-emergency)
255 W. Dundee Rd.   847/459-2632

Fire Department (non-emergency)
255 W. Dundee Rd.   847/459-2662

Police, Fire, and Ambulance (emergency)   911

Townships

Vernon Township
2050 N. Main St.
Buffalo Grove   847/634-4600

Wheeling Township
1616 N. Arlington Heights Rd.
Arlington Heights   847/259-7730

Parks and Recreation

Wheeling Park District
Community Recreation Center
333 W. Dundee Rd.   847/465-3333

Libraries

Indian Trails Public Library
355 S. Schoenbeck Rd.   847/459-4100

Vernon Area Public Library
300 Olde Half Day Rd.
Lincolnshire   847/634-3650

Schools

School Districts

Community Consolidated District 21
999 W. Dundee Rd.   847/537-8270

High School District 214
2121 S. Goebbert Rd.
Arlington Heights   847/437-4600

Community Colleges

Harper College
1200 W. Algonquin Rd.
Palatine   847/925-6000

Selected Community Organizations

Wheeling Community Resource Center
54 N. Wolf Rd.   847/808-1454

Wheeling Historical Society
P.O. Box 3
Wheeling, IL 60090   847/537-3119

251 N. Wolf Rd. (museum)
Chamber Park   847/537-3119

Houses of Worship

Antioch Bible Church
480 S. Elmhurst Rd.   847/537-9632

Calvary Presbyterian Church
704 Old McHenry Rd.   847/459-3080

Community Presbyterian Church
196 Highland Ave.   847/537-4449

First Baptist Church
1507 Cedarwood Ln.   847/259-7613

Iglesia Bautista El Buen
624 Old McHenry Rd.   847/215-0306

Our Savior Evangelical Free Church
300 Schoenbeck Rd.   847/459-4440

Reaching Indians Ministries (East Indian)
18 Schoenbeck Rd.   847/215-2827

St. Joseph the Worker
171 W. Dundee Rd.   847/537-4181

Congregation Beth Am (Reform)
850 Jenkins Ct.   847/459-1677

Congregation Beth Judea (Conservative)
Rt. 83 and Hilltop Rd.
Long Grove   847/634-0777

Congregation B'nai Shalom (Traditional)
701 W. Aptakisic Rd.
Buffalo Grove   847/541-1460

Congregation Mishpaha (Reform)
Call for meeting place.   847/459-3279

Congregation Shirat Emet (Reform)
Call for meeting place.　　　　　　　　847/541-7273

Lubavitch Chabad (Orthodox)
16296 W. Aptakisic Rd.
Prairie View　　　　　　　　　　　　847/808-7770

Project Seed of Suburban Chicago (Orthodox)
158 McHenry Rd.
Buffalo Grove　　　　　　　　　　　847/215-7664

Temple Chai (Reform)
1670 Checker Rd.
Long Grove　　　　　　　　　　　　847/537-1771

Temple Shir Shalom (Reform)
325 Lexington Dr.
Buffalo Grove　　　　　　　　　　　847/465-0101

DINING

The Restaurants of Restaurant Row

Officially, Wheeling's "Restaurant Row" covers the almost two miles between Palatine Expressway and Lake-Cook Road on Milwaukee Avenue. Unofficially, there are a couple of restaurants north of Lake-Cook Road that should also be included—namely, Han's Bavarian Lodge, Daniello's, and The Weber Grill (see "Native's Choices" on p. 66).

Hackney's, Bob Chinn's, Le Francais, and Golden Chef were really the first on the block, so to speak, and it's probably due to their popularity that village officials were able to entice so many new restaurants. The recent completion of road work along Milwaukee Avenue has made all of these great restaurants much easier to find.

Bob Chinn's Crabhouse
393 S. Milwaukee Ave.
847/843-2722
Need seafood? Stop looking. Bob Chinn's has the freshest fish around, bar none. The daily flight records posted on the wall as you enter this mammoth restaurant proves it: Bob Chinn has his fish flown in daily from around the world. Chinn himself often visits tables to make sure everyone is content. They are.
Open for lunch Mon. - Fri. 11 a.m. - 2:30 p.m., Sat. - Sun. 12 p.m. - 3 p.m.; for dinner Mon. - Thurs. 4:30 p.m. - 10:30 p.m., Fri. 4:30 p.m. - 11:30 p.m., Sat. 3 p.m. - 11:30 p.m., Sun. 3 p.m. - 10 p.m.

Buca di Beppo
604 N. Milwaukee Ave.
847/808-9898
Whoever conceived of this place was an absolute glutton. Like at its counterpart on Chicago's Clark Street, portions are enormous (enough to feed *at least* two people) and prices are downright cheap, making the hearty Italian specialties irresistible. This is one of the only places I'll actually recommend ordering chicken. The atmosphere is lively and *kitschy*, with countless photographs and memorabilia covering the walls. It can be noisy at times, but that's part of the fun. Prices range from $8.95 to $18.95.
Open Mon. - Thurs. 5 p.m. - 10 p.m., Fri. 5 p.m. - 11 p.m., Sat. 4 p.m. - 11 p.m., Sun. 4 p.m. - 11 p.m.

Buona Sera Cucina Italiana
102 S. Milwaukee Ave.
847/229-0404.
Yet another excellent entry in the Italian cuisine market, although the interior and the menu are a bit more refined than Buca di Beppo (see p. 65), listed above. Prices range from $9.95 to about $17.95. All of the pasta dishes are excellent, but the veal is to die for.
Open for lunch daily 11 a.m. - 2:30 p.m.; for dinner Sun. - Thurs. 5 p.m. - 9 p.m., Fri. - Sat. 5 p.m. - 10:30 p.m.

Crawdaddy Bayou
412 N. Milwaukee Ave.
847/520-4800
After a trip or two to New Orleans, I developed a fondness for Southern cooking, mudbugs, and Zydeco music. Since then, Crawdaddy Bayou in Wheeling substantially reduced my road-trip time. All of the

above, and more, can be found inside these swamp-themed walls. This is one of my favorite places to just kick back and hang out, especially when there's a band in the bar Thursday through Sunday.
Open for lunch Tues. - Sun. 11:30 a.m. - 2:30 p.m.; for dinner Tues. - Thurs. 5 p.m. - 10 p.m., Fri. - Sat. 5 p.m. - 11 p.m., Sun. 4 p.m. - 9 p.m. Closed Mon.

Don Roth's in Wheeling
61 N. Milwaukee Ave.
847/537-5800
There's a lot of history here, from the 1800s building to the traditional prime rib and beef cuts made from a recipe developed in the 1920s at the original Blackhawk Restaurant in Chicago. The atmosphere is family-rustic. Prices are slightly above average, but generally worth it. Service is excellent.
Open for lunch Mon. - Fri. 11:30 a.m. - 2 p.m.; for dinner Mon. - Thurs. 5:30 p.m. - 9:30 p.m., Fri. 5:30 p.m. - 10:30 p.m., Sat. 5 p.m. - 10:30 p.m., Sun. 4 p.m. - 8:30 p.m.

Le Francais
269 S. Milwaukee Ave.
847/541-7470
For many years Le Francais has maintained a four-star rating based on its truly exceptional, traditional French cuisine and stellar wine list. During the printing of this guide, the restaurant is expected to close for remodeling and some menu changes. We can only assume the owners will maintain the fine traditions. Prices are high; expect to spend around $100 per person.
Call for hours.

Golden Chef Restaurant
600 S. Milwaukee Ave.
847/537-7100
This is much more than your average Chinese take-out place. While the interior of the restaurant is modest, the food is anything but, with Cantonese and Szechuan dishes made with health in mind; the owner is a nutritionist. Service is very attentive and prices are very, very affordable; they haven't changed for more than ten years.
Open daily 11:30 a.m. - 9:30 p.m.

Hackney's
241 S. Milwaukee Ave.
847/537-2100
This long-time favorite family restaurant is the real stand-by of most locals. Meals range from burgers to steaks and fish, the atmosphere is very friendly, and prices are easy on the pocketbook. For an appetizer, try the popular onion loaf, order it in a half-size for two. The burgers are the best in the suburbs.
Open Mon. - Sat. 11:15 a.m. - 10: 30 p.m., Sun. 12 p.m. - 10:30 p.m.

Native's Choices

See also "Restaurant Row" in this chapter on p. 63.

Daniello's
913 N. Milwaukee Ave.
847/459-7200
Daniello's country Italian food is excellent, and everyone raves about the bread; you can even take a loaf or two home. But I'm going to skip right to dessert. Order the tiramisu. You will never want to order it anywhere else. Locals love the place, as well they should; it's been around for almost 20 years.
Open daily for lunch 11 a.m. - 4 p.m., daily for dinner 4 p.m. - 10 p.m.

Han's Bavarian Lodge
931 N. Milwaukee Ave.
847/537-4141
I'll admit right up front that I have something of a bias for Han's food—my wife and I held our rehearsal dinner in the upstairs banquet room. But considering how many restaurants I've covered on the dining beat, you have to figure we had good reason. The traditional German menu is exceptional and goes down even better with a cold weiss beer or any of Berghoff's brews. Prices generally fall in the mid-teens. Don't miss the phenomenal Oktoberfest, which usually takes place over several weekends beginning in mid-September.
Open Tues. - Thurs. 11:30 a.m. - 9:45 p.m., Fri. 11:30 a.m. - 10:45 p.m., Sat. 4 p.m. - 10:45 p.m., Sun. 12 p.m. - 9 p.m.

Taste of Hunan
1 Huntington Ln.
847/419-0698.
Traditional Szechuan and Hunan specialties are prepared to order with the freshest ingredients. This is definitely above-average Chinese food, and service is almost motherly. Eat in or take-out.
Open daily 11 a.m. - 9:30 p.m.

The Country Cupboard—one of the many scenic shops in Long Grove.

LONG GROVE

Long Grove at a Glance
Incorporated: 1956
Population: 6,058
Median Household Income: $218,893
Median Home Value: $500,000

Long Grove has the distinction of being one of the most beautiful villages in the Northwest Suburbs. Houses and properties are large, well maintained, and on the pricier end of the scale; but the trade-offs are numerous, including the fact that residents pay no local property taxes. Instead, the village draws its revenues primarily from the stunning historic downtown businesses, as well as the large headquarters of Kemper Insurance.

Downtown Long Grove is something of a local wonder, with buildings dating back to the earliest days of the village (it was settled in 1838) and much of the atmosphere of days gone by. The retail base is made up of art galleries, antique stores, and specialty shops, and while there are plenty of beautiful things to buy, it's not likely one will find any of those antiques under-priced.

Still, there is almost no season that is immune from Long Grove's charms. In winter, one can stroll the streets snacking on roasted chestnuts purchased from a wizened and friendly street vendor, sip hot chocolate, and listen to choirs singing Christmas carols a cappella. Summer months boast a number of weekend festivals, including the Strawberry Festival, when vendors line the streets with virtually every strawberry creation imaginable, from preserves to a fiery strawberry hot sauce.

The other part of Long Grove's beauty lies outside the boundaries of downtown in the open, natural areas that act as buffers between homes and developments. The population of the village is around 5,500, but it would be difficult to guess that by driving down any of the major streets.

Long Grove was incorporated in 1956, and like neighboring villages Hawthorn Woods and Kildeer, it was founded in an aggressive attempt to defend the surrounding environment and desired atmosphere of the village against encroaching development. The effort was successful; today, thick, mature trees line almost every street that isn't bordered by open fields and marshes. Even if you avoid shopping altogether, it's a nice place to take a short afternoon drive.

ESSENTIAL CONTACTS

Basics

Long Grove Village Hall 3110 RFD	847/634-9440
Long Grove Merchants Association	847/634-0888
Police (non-emergency) Lake County Sheriff	847/549-5200
Fire and Paramedics (non-emergency) Countryside Fire Protection District Long Grove Fire Protection District	847/367-5511 847/634-3142
Police, Fire, and Ambulance (emergency)	911

Townships

Vernon Township 2050 N. Main St. Buffalo Grove	847/634-4600

Parks and Recreation

Long Grove Park District	847/438-4743

Libraries

Ela Area Public Library
135 S. Buesching Rd.
Lake Zurich   847/438-3433

Vernon Area Public Library
300 Olde Half Day Rd.
Lincolnshire   847/634-3650

Schools

School Districts

Diamond Lake School District 76
500 Acorn Ln.
Diamond Lake   847/566-9221

Fremont School District 79
28855 N. Fremont Center Rd.   847/566-0169

Kildeer-Countryside Elementary District 96
777 Checker Dr.
Buffalo Grove   847/459-4260

Stevenson High School District 125
1 Stevenson Dr.
Lincolnshire   847/634-4000

Community Colleges

College of Lake County (community college)
19351 W. Washington St.
Grayslake   847/233-6601

Harper College
1200 W. Algonquin Rd.
Palatine   847/925-6000

DINING

Native's Choices

Because Long Grove is a tourist attraction, store and restaurant hours vary substantially, depending on the season. Call in advance regardless of whether reservations are required.

Village Tavern
135 Mchenry Rd.
847/634-3117
It would be difficult to find a restaurant anywhere quite like the Village Tavern. The food (roadhouse-style burgers, meat-and-potatoes dinners) and service (always with a smile) are great, in spite of the large number of people who visit every day. Prices are very affordable ($5.95-$14.95), and the tavern portion of the large restaurant can be a welcome respite from a long day of shopping. Then again, *everything* here—antiques and collectibles line the walls—is for sale. Don't miss the enormous grandfather clock in the bar or the weekly auctions.
Kitchen open Mon. 11:30 a.m. - 9 p.m., Tues. - Sun. 11:30 a.m. - 10 p.m.; bar open daily 11:30 a.m. - 12 a.m.

Worth Noting

Seasons of Long Grove
314 Old McHenry Rd.
847/634-9150
The floral, teahouse atmosphere makes this a pleasant spot for a light lunch (served buffet-style) or Sunday brunch. Dress is slightly better than casual, especially when high tea is served between 2:30 p.m. - 4 p.m. Prices from about $9.95 to $15.95.
Open Mon. - Sat. 11 a.m. - 2:30 p.m., Sun. brunch 10 a.m. - 2 p.m.

PROSPECT HEIGHTS

Prospect Heights at a Glance
Incorporated: 1976
Population: 15,280
Median Household Income: $60,197
Median Home Value: $237,229

The city began as an unincorporated area in Cook County in 1935, when Carlton Smith and Allen Dawson built a group of homes on farm property near Elmhurst Road.

It wasn't until 1976, however, when a spurt of development occurred throughout the suburbs, that the City of Prospect Heights was officially incorporated.

Tucked between Wheeling and Mount Prospect (each of which share park districts and libraries with the city), Prospect Heights qualifies as a bedroom community due to its limited business base.

ESSENTIAL CONTACTS

Basics

City of Prospect Heights (City Hall)
14 E. Camp McDonald Rd.   847/398-6070

Wheeling/Prospect Heights Area Chamber of Commerce
395 E. Dundee Rd.
Wheeling   847/541-0170

Police Department (non-emergency)
14 E. Camp McDonald Rd.   847/398-5511

Fire Department (non-emergency)
10 E. Camp McDonald Rd.   847/253-8060

Police, Fire, and Ambulance (emergency)   911

Townships

Wheeling Township
1616 N. Arlington Heights Rd.
Arlington Heights   847/259-7730

Parks and Recreation

Prospect Heights Park District
110 W. Camp McDonald Rd.   847/394-2848

River Trails Park District
1313 Burning Bush Ln.
Mount Prospect   847/298-4445

Wheeling Park District
333 W. Dundee Rd.
Wheeling   847/465-7760

Libraries

Indian Trails Public Library
355 S. Schoenbeck Rd.
Wheeling   847/459-4100

Prospect Heights Library District
12 N. Elm St.
Prospect Heights   847/259-3500

Schools

School Districts

Community Consolidated School District 21
999 W. Dundee Rd.
Wheeling   847/537-8270

Prospect Heights School District 23
700 N. Schoenbeck Rd.   847/870-3875

River Trails School District 26
1900 Kensington Rd.
Mount Prospect   847/870-3850

School District 214
2121 S. Goebbert Rd.
Arlington Heights   847/718-7600

Selected Community Organizations

See listings in *Wheeling*, p. 61.

Houses of Worship

Church of the Good Shepherd
1111 N. Elmhurst Rd.   847/537-4353

Hebron Presbyterian Church
511 N. Schoenbeck Rd.   847/394-8454

Korean Central United Methodist Church
203 E. Camp McDonald Rd.   847/797-1144

Northwest Bible Baptist Church
203 E. Camp McDonald Rd.   847/577-4512

Our Redeemer Lutheran Church
304 W. Palatine Rd.   847/537-4430

Propect Christian Church
302 E. Euclid Ave.   847/398-2030

Prospect Heights Baptist Church
308 E. Camp McDonald Rd.   847/255-1394

Prospect Heights Community Church
400 N. Elmhurst Rd.   847/253-2772

Renacer Baptist Church
304 W. Palatine Rd.   847/459-4842

St. Alphonsus Catholic Church
411 N. Wheeling Rd.   847/255-5538

St. Hilary's Episcopal Church
307 W. Hintz Rd.   847/537-0590

The Great Work Korean Church
308 E. Camp McDonald Rd.   847/590-1432

DES PLAINES
AND
MOUNT
PROSPECT

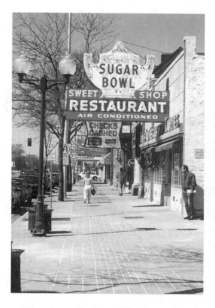

Blast from the Past: The Sugar Bowl
Restaurant in Des Plaines.

Prospect Heights, Mount Prospect, Des Plaines, and Rosemont

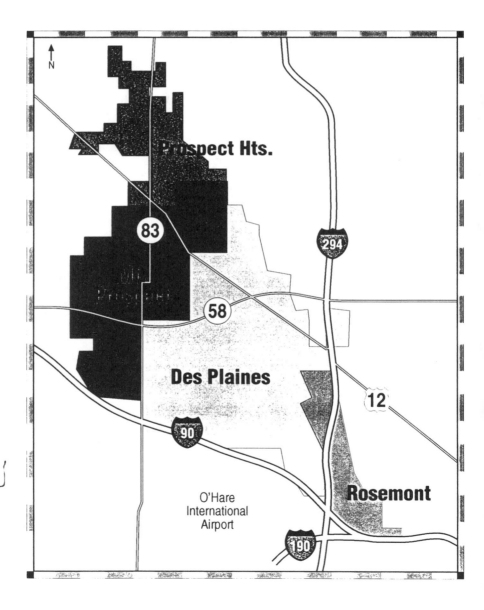

DES PLAINES

Des Plaines at a Glance

Incorporated: 1869
Population: 54,836
Median Household Income: $60,621
Median Home Value: $172,500

In spite of its prime location and venerable history, the downtown business district of Des Plaines has suffered a sort of identity crisis in recent years. Most of that is simply growing pains. Local leaders tend to agree that the downtown needs a face-lift, as well as a sense of character that might provide a competitive edge over the neighboring villages of Mount Prospect and Park Ridge.

Still, housing prices are relatively affordable, schools are good, recreational opportunities are plentiful, and the village's proximity to O'Hare International Airport and major transportation corridors give the village a ton of potential.

The Des Plaines River once served as a conduit to bring the earliest settlers to the area. Today's travelers are more likely to be bicyclists and joggers treading down the Des Plaines River Trail, which cuts directly through the community.

In addition to a handful of historic homes and the 1906 Benjamin F. Kinder House (a historic museum), Des Plaines boasts the McDonald's #1 Store Museum, a re-creation of the first McDonald's Restaurant franchise opened April 15, 1955.

Its downtown movie theater is also a throwback to earlier times, and recent renovations to the site guarantee it will last for generations to come.

Des Plaines is also home to what may be the finest community theater in the area. The Bog Theater regularly produces exceptional plays for adults and children at rock-bottom prices; if there's a show on the boards, catch it.

ESSENTIAL CONTACTS

Basics

The City of Des Plaines
1420 Miner St.   847/391-5300

Chamber of Commerce & Industry
1401 Oakton St.   847/824-4200

Police Department
1420 Miner St.   847/391-5400

Fire Department
405 S. River Rd. (Station One)   847/391-5356

Townships

Elk Grove Township
2400 S. Arlington Heights Rd.
Arlington Heights   847/437-0300

Maine Township
1700 Ballard Rd.
Park Ridge   847/297-2510

Wheeling Township
1616 N. Arlington Heights Rd.
Arlington Heights   847/259-7730

Parks and Recreation

Des Plaines Park District
2222 Birch St.   847/391-5700

Des Plaines Park District Community Concert Band
1800 Stewart Ave.   847/391-5711

Mt. Prospect Park District
411 S. Maple St.
Mount Prospect   847/255-5380

Libraries

Des Plaines Public Library
841 Graceland Ave.   847/827-5551

Schools

School Districts

Community Consolidated School District 26
1900 E. Kensington Rd.
Mt. Prospect   847/297-4120

Community Consolidated School District 59
2123 S. Arlington Heights Rd.
Arlington Heights   847/593-4300

Des Plaines Community Consolidated School District 62
777 Algonquin Rd.   847/824-1136

High School District 214
2121 S. Goebbert Rd.
Arlington Heights   847/437-4600

Maine Township High School District 207
1131 S. Dee Rd.
Park Ridge   847/696-3600

School District 63
10150 Dee Rd.   847/299-1900

Private Elementary Schools

Brentwood Baptist Christian Academy
588 Dara James Rd.   847/298-3399

Creative Children's Academy
500 N. Benton St.
Palatine   847/202-8035

Immanuel Lutheran School
832 Lee St.   847/824-4405

Our Lady of Destiny School (North Campus)
795 Center St.   847/824-2762

Our Lady of Destiny School (South Campus)
1880 Ash St.   847/827-2900

St. Zachary's Catholic School
567 W. Algonquin Rd.   847/437-4022

Science and Arts Academy
1825 Miner St.   847/827-7880

Willows Academy
1012 Thacker St.   847/824-6900

Private High Schools

Willows Academy
1012 Thacker St.   847/824-6900

Community Colleges

Harper College
1200 W. Algonquin Rd.
Palatine   847/397-3000

Oakton Community College
1600 E. Golf Rd.   847/635-1600

Roosevelt University
Schaumburg Campus
1651 McConnor Pkwy.
Schaumburg   847/619-8600

Selected Community Organizations

American Association of Retired Persons (AARP)
Prairie Lakes Community Center
515 E. Thacker St.   847/391-5717

Center of Concern
1580 N. Northwest Hwy.
Park Ridge   847/823-0453

Des Plaines Arts Council
1755 S. Wolf Rd.   847/391-5700

Des Plaines Camera Club
820 Graceland Ave., #303   847/696-2899

Des Plaines Community Senior Center
515 E. Thacker St.   847/391-5717

Des Plaines Garden Club
515 E. Thacker St.   847/824-3875

Des Plaines Police Youth Clubs
1420 Miner St.   847/391-5400

Des Plaines Theater Guild
P. O. Box 84
Des Plaines, IL 60016   847/391-5720

Des Plaines Valley Geological Society
214 N. Broadway Ave.
Park Ridge   847/823-0634

Historical Society of Des Plaines
789 Pearson St.   847/391-5399

Lattof International YMCA
300 E. Northwest Hwy.   847/296-3376

Life Span
P.O. Box 445   847/824-0382

Maine Center for Mental Health
832 Busse Hwy.
Park Ridge   847/696-1570

Maine Township Seniors (Options 55 & 1+ Options)
1700 Ballard Rd.
Park Ridge   847/297-2510

Maine-Niles Association of Special Recreation (M-NASR)
8950 Gross Point Rd., Ste. C
Skokie   847/966-5522

New Resident Service
1401 Oakton St.   847/824-4200

Optimist Club of Des Plaines
P. O. Box 1547   847/821-1272

Parents Who Care
P.O. Box 68631
Schaumburg   630/483-0637

Photographic Art & Science Foundation, Inc.
111 Stratford Rd.   847/824-6855

Salvation Army
The Community Counseling Center
609 W. Dempster St.   847/981-9113

Special People, Inc.
1420 Miner St., Rm. #302   847/827-1893

Welcome Wagon
309 E. Niagara Ave.
Schaumburg   847/985-9266

Houses of Worship

Alliance Bible Church
382 S. Mt. Prospect Rd.   847/299-4201

Brentwood Baptist Church
588 Dara James   847/298-3399

Calvary Korean Baptist Church
1575 S. Wolf Rd.   847/297-8190

Chicago Marthoma Episcopal Church
240 Potter Rd.   847/296-4624

Christ Church (United Church of Christ)
1492 Henry Ave.   847/297-4230

Des Plaines Bible Church
946 E. Thacker St.   847/297-2525

Des Plaines Church of Christ
1794 Illinois St.   847/824-8200

Evangelical Free Church of Des Plaines
55 W. Golf Rd.   847/635-7776

Faith Bible Church
355 S. Bellaire Ave.   847/298-4197

First Church of Christian Scientist
1275 Marion St.   847/824-1904

First Congregational Church
766 Graceland Ave.   847/299-5561

First Presbyterian Church of Des Plaines
1755 Howard Ave.   847/299-4215

First United Methodist Church
666 Graceland Ave.   847/827-5561

Golf Road Baptist Church
501 W. Golf Rd.   847/439-0276

Good News Community Church
700 Pearson St.   847/390-5840

Good Shepherd Lutheran Church
1177 E. Howard Ave.   847/824-4923

Hna Presbyterian Church
1485 Whitcomb Ave.   847/803-1131

Holy Virgin Protection Cathedral
1800 Lee St.   847/824-0971

Immanuel Community Baptist Church
1969 Touhy Ave.   847/803-3406

Immanuel Lutheran Church
855 Lee St.   847/824-3652

Maine Township Jewish Congregation Shaare Emet
8800 Ballard Rd.   847/297-2006

Phat Bao Buddhist Temple
1495 Prospect Ave.   847/827-4599

St. John the Baptist Greek Orthodox Church
2350 E. Dempster St.   847/827-5519

St. Martin's Episcopal Church
1095 E. Thacker St.   847/824-2043

St. Stephen Catholic Church
1253 Everett Ave.   847/297-3844

St. Stephen's Catholic Church
1280 Prospect Ave.   847/824-2026

St. Zachary Catholic Church
567 W. Algonquin Rd.   847/956-7020

Trinity Lutheran Church
675 E. Algonquin Rd.   847/827-6656

United Evangelical Church
2247 University St.   847/299-4466

United Pentecostal Church
1280 E. Algonquin Rd.   847/299-7729

Unity Northwest Church
259 E. Central Rd.   847/297-4137

DINING

Native's Choices

Cafe La Cave
2777 Mannheim Rd.
847/827-7818
This is arguably Des Plaines' finest restaurant, featuring elegant and indulgent cuisine in a setting reminiscent of the Palace of Versailles. The rack of lamb is outstanding, as is any salmon dish. Entrees start at $19.95.
Open for lunch Mon. - Fri. 11:30 a.m. - 3 p.m., for dinner daily 5 p.m. - 10 p.m.

D'Nunzios Ristorante Italiano
740 N. Wolf Rd.
847/390-7330
If you can get out of here without increasing your belt size, you just haven't experienced D'Nunzio's at its best. The food is true country Italian, served in heaping portions with attention to quality. The *Braciola Zi Pascuale* is excellent, as is the *Baccala Sorrentino*. Prices range from $9.95 to about $18.95.
Open Mon. - Thurs. 11 a.m. - 10 p.m., Fri. 11 a.m. - 12 a.m., Sat. 4 p.m. - 12 a.m., Sun. 4 p.m. - 10 p.m.

Worth Noting

Black Ram
1414 E. Oakton St.
847/824-1227
This place seems like it's been around forever. It draws a consistent group of regulars and is popular with the older business executive crowd. The selection of food is mostly intimidating—rack of lamb and steaks are the best bet, and the wine list is more than worthy. Prices are still on the low end, from around $9.95 to $17.95.
Open Mon. - Fri. 11 a.m. - 12 a.m., Sat. 4 p.m. - 1 a.m., Sun. 1 p.m. - 10 p.m.

Crab & Things
1249 S. Elmhurst Rd.
847/437-1595
A dozen raw oysters for less than $10 is the first reason to visit this hidden gem; you'll come back for the friendly crowd and casual feel. Prices range from about $12.95 to $15.95 for entrees.
Open for lunch Mon. - Fri. 11:30 a.m. - 3:30 p.m.; for dinner Sun. - Thurs. 3 p.m. - 10 p.m., Fri. - Sat. 3 p.m. - 11 p.m.

Kuhn's Delicatessen
749 W. Golf Rd.
847/640-0222
For top-quality German sausages and cheeses, you'll not find a better or more well-stocked deli than Kuhn's anywhere. Though not really a dining establishment, a large selection of gourmet delicacies, mustards, and the like make this a great place for a sandwich on the run.
Open Sun. - Fri. 10 a.m. - 7 p.m., Sat. 9 a.m. - 7 p.m.

Sugar Bowl Sweet Shop and Restaurant
1494 Miner St.
847/824-7380
The food itself is slightly better-than-average breakfast and burger fare served fast, hot, and cheap. But it's the atmosphere that will keep you coming back. The interior harkens to the days of soda jerks and hoop skirts and makes a good case for the possibility of time travel.
Open daily 6 a.m. - 3 p.m.

MOUNT PROSPECT

Mount Prospect at a Glance

Incorporated: 1917
Population: 54,040
Median Household Income: $67,500
Median Home Value: $197,800

Mount Prospect is a large but close-knit community that has preserved much of its history in the neighborhoods and downtown business district that straddle Northwest Highway.

The first railroad station was built around 1875, at the urging of Ezra Eggleston, a developer and early settler in the area. The railway was really the lifeblood of virtually all of the northwest communities and is responsible in many ways for the various population booms throughout the years. Today, Mount Prospect's population is nearly 54,000, with average single-family home prices near $200,000 and above.

An active historical society offers a number of events throughout the year, including an Antique and Specialty Auto Show held in late summer, a holiday historic house-walk during the Christmas season, and various monthly programs and shows. Most of the events take place at the Dietrich Friedrichs House and Museum (101 S. Maple St.), a classic example of early 20th century Victorian architecture.

A number of businesses contribute to the village's economy, most notable among which is the Randhurst Shopping Center, boasting almost 150 stores (see *Shopping*, p. 244). Searle and NutraSweet Kelco Co. also make their homes here.

The gem of the local park district is the Mount Prospect RecPlex, one of the finest recreational facilities in the area, featuring a large pool, fitness center, and racquetball courts.

The small, but beautifully maintained Friendship Park Conservatory offers a number of nature programs for children and adults, but also makes a wonderful and inexpensive location for small parties and wedding receptions (a fact to which I can attest first-hand).

ESSENTIAL CONTACTS

Basics

Village of Mount Prospect
100 S. Emerson St.   847/392-6000

Mount Prospect Chamber of Commerce
111 E. Busse Ave.   847/398-6616

Police Department (non-emergency)
112 E. Northwest Hwy.   847/870-5666

Fire Department (non-emergency)
112 E. Northwest Hwy.   847/870-5656

Police, Fire, and Ambulance (emergency)   911

Townships

Elk Grove Township
2400 S. Arlington Heights Rd.
Arlington Heights   847/437-0300

Wheeling Township
1616 N. Arlington Heights Rd.
Arlington Heights   847/259-7730

Parks and Recreation

Friendship Park Conservatory
395 Algonquin Rd.   847/298-3500

Lions Recreation Center
411 S. Maple St.   847/632-9333

Mount Prospect Park District
1000 W. Central Rd.   847/255-5380

RecPlex
420 W. Dempster St.   847/640-1000

Senior Center
50 S. Emerson St.   847/870-5680

Libraries

Mount Prospect Public Library
10 S. Emerson St.   847/253-5675

Schools

School Districts

Elk Grove District 59
2123 S. Arlington Heights Rd.
Arlington Heights   847/593-4300

Mount Prospect School District 57
701 W. Gregory   847/394-7300

River Trails District 26
1900 E. Kensington Rd.   847/297-4120

Township High School District 214
2121 S. Goebbert Rd.
Arlington Heights   847/437-4600

Wheeling Township District 21
999 W. Dundee Rd.
Wheeling   847/537-8270

Community Colleges

Harper College
1200 W. Algonquin Rd.
Palatine   847/925-6000

Selected Community Organizations

Community Development Department
100 S. Emerson St.   847/818-5328

Greater Woodfield Convention and Visitors Bureau
1375 Woodfield Rd., Ste. 100
Schaumburg   847/605-1010

Mount Prospect Historical Society
Dietrich Friedrichs House
101 S. Maple St.   847/392-9006

Prospect Heights Convention and Visitors Bureau
7 N. Elmhurst Rd.
Prospect Heights   847/577-3666

Houses of Worship

Bible Baptist Church
123 S. Busse Rd.   847/593-3612

Christian Life Church
400 E. Gregory St.   847/259-3090

Community Presbyterian Church
407 N. Main St.   847/392-3111

Cumberland Baptist Church
1500 E. Central Rd.   847/296-3242

Lutheran Church of Martha and Mary
606 W. Golf Rd.   847/259-2568

Mount Prospect Bible Church
505 W. Golf Rd.   847/439-3337

New Life Apostolic Faith Church
1 W. Euclid Ave.   847/259-8107

New Life Christian Center
209 S. Hi Lusi St.   847/506-9673

Northwest Assembly of God Church
900 N. Wolf Rd.   847/299-2400

Peace Church
2090 W. Golf Rd.   847/228-1420

St. John Lutheran Church
1100 S. Linneman Rd.   847/593-7670

St. Mark Lutheran Church
200 S. Wille St.   847/253-0631

St. Paul Lutheran Church
100 S. School St.   847/255-0332

Trinity United Methodist Church
605 W. Golf Rd.   847/398-3806

DINING

Native's Choices

Dumas Walker's
1799 S. Busse Rd.
847/593-2200
Mount Prospect meets Texas in this enormous country bar and eatery.
This is the only place east of the Mississippi with a dance floor the
size of a football field...and with enough friendly faces to fill it. Even if
you don't know how to line dance, you can learn how to here without
feeling like a fool. The food is decent and cheap and will give you

enough energy to dance the night away. Weekends can be crowded—Dumas Walker's seems to have come out of the country craze as a true survivor.

Open Mon. - Thurs. 11 a.m. - 1 a.m., Fri. 11 a.m. - 2 a.m., Sat. 4 p.m. - 2 a.m., Sun. 4 p.m. - 10 p.m.

Mrs. P and Me
100 E. Prospect Ave.
847/259-9724

This family-owned favorite has everything going for it. The interior is casual and comfortable, the staff is friendly as can be, the American food is always reliable, and prices won't bowl you over. (Few entrees fall above $10.) On weekends, the focus shifts from the restaurant to the bar, where you'll find plenty of friendly locals willing to tip a drink or two.

Kitchen open Mon. - Thurs. 11 a.m. - 9:30 p.m., Fri. - Sat. 11 a.m. - 10:30 p.m., Sun. 12 p.m. - 10 p.m.; bar open Mon. - Thurs. until 1 a.m., Fri. - Sat. until 2 a.m.

Ye Olde Town Inn
18 W. Busse Ave.
847/392-3750

It's fair to say that if the locals aren't at Mrs. P & Me (see above listing), they're either here or in bed. Ye Olde Town Inn has a slightly more limited bar menu, but that's made up for in atmosphere and live music on weekends. Food is impossibly cheap; just try to beat the 16-oz. porterhouse for $4.95 (honest) and complimentary appetizers from 4 p.m. to 6 p.m. Dart boards (cork and electronic) and pool tables stay full on weekends. This is the kind of place that regulars don't want anyone else to know about.

Open Mon. - Thurs. 12 p.m. - 1 a.m., Fri. 12 p.m. - 2 a.m., Sat. 3 p.m. - 2 a.m., Sun. 3 p.m. - 9 p.m.

Worth Noting

Cuisine of India Restaurant
2348 S. Elmhurst Rd.
847/718-1522

There are a surprising number of good Indian restaurants in the suburbs (see *Schaumburg*, p. 153), but this one ranks among the best. Dishes

with carefully balanced spices are made to order, ingredients are fresh, and service is top-notch. Prices range from about $7.95 to $11.95.
Open for lunch caily 11:30 a.m. - 3 p.m.; for dinner served daily 5 p.m. - 10 p.m.

El Sombrero
1100 S. Elmhurst Rd.
847/364-0030
El Sombrero is one of the more popular and long-lasting of the Mexican restaurant choices around. The menu features a range of authentic traditional cuisine. If you're hungry, order a large steak burrito and wash it down with a margarita or two. Prices are quite reasonable, from about $6.95 to $12.95.
Kitchen open Mon. - Thurs. 11 a.m. - 9:30 p.m., Fri. - Sat. 11 a.m. - 12 a.m., Sun. 12 p.m. - 9:30 p.m.; bar open Mon. - Thurs. until 1 a.m., Fri. - Sat. until 2 a.m.

Gail's Carriage Inn Pancake House
401 E. Euclid Ave., 847/368-1228
20 W. Northwest Hwy., 847/255-5454
How can a restaurant be so good as to warrant two locations in the same town? Stop in one morning for the pancakes, omelets, or just a cup of java, and you'll find out. Figure on a crowd during the morning rush—you'll still be treated well.
Open Mon. - Fri. 6 a.m. - 3 p.m., Sat. - Sun. 7 a.m. - 3 p.m.

Kampai Japanese Steak House
2330 S. Elmhurst Rd.
847/640-6700
The lively atmosphere and fresh ingredients (not to mention the "floating" sushi bar) make this one of the more popular of the "prepared-at-your-table" steak houses. Prices are reasonable, around $20 for most entrees, which includes everything from appetizer to dessert. Try the Kampai special or sirloin and lobster if you don't want sushi.
Open for lunch Tues. - Fri. 11:30 a.m. - 2 p.m.; for dinner Mon. - Thurs. 5:30 p.m. - 9:30 p.m., Fri. - Sat. 5:30 p.m. - 10 p.m., Sun. 5 p.m. - 9 p.m.

ELK GROVE
VILLAGE
AND
ROSEMONT

Rosemont's colorful water tower has a
red and pink top and a green base.

ELK GROVE VILLAGE

Elk Grove Village at a Glance

Incorporated: 1957
Population: 34,470
Median Household Income: $70,113
Median Home Value: $186,700

One of the first of the "planned communities" of the 1950s, Elk Grove Village began as a quiet rural outpost with only 130 residents.

Around 1941, property bordering the village was owned by Douglas Aircraft, a company which built military planes. The land was sold to the City of Chicago in 1946 and became the Orchard Place Airport. (Thus, the "ORD" still seen on O'Hare's baggage tags.)

It wasn't long before the airport was renamed O'Hare, after local World War II hero Butch O'Hare.

Financially, Elk Grove could only benefit from its proximity to the airport. Urban planners designed the village to be comprised of half industrial and half residential uses, with easy access to schools, parks, and churches.

A drive down any of the busy thoroughfares in town makes the term "easy access" somewhat relative. The industrial aspect of the village is obvious enough, and there is a strong hotel and retail presence. Discovery of the quieter residential neighborhoods requires getting off the main streets.

Until recently, Elk Grove was lacking a "heart"—a central place in the community. That changed with the redevelopment of Town Square, which features businesses and a park where residents gather for festivities such as the annual Christmas tree-lighting ceremony.

Village leaders have also made concerted efforts to provide recreational facilities for residents of all ages. In 1998, park district officials met with a group of high school students who designed their own skateboarding facility, which is scheduled for construction over the next year or so.

The park district also recently built a 110,000-square-foot pavilion, housing two indoor and two outdoor swimming pools, two gyms, racquetball courts, and a fitness center, among other things. It serves as one of the primary gathering points for residents of the community.

ESSENTIAL CONTACTS

Basics

Village of Elk Grove Village
901 Wellington Ave.   847/439-3900

Greater O'Hare Association (chamber of commerce)
1050 Busse Rd., Ste. 100
Bensenville   630/350-2944

Police Department (non-emergency)
901 Wellington Ave.   847/439-3900

Fire Department (non-emergency)
901 Wellington Ave.   847/439-3900

Police, Fire, and Ambulance (emergency)   911

Townships

Addison Township
401 N. Addison Rd.
Addison   630/530-8161

Elk Grove Township
2400 S. Arlington Heights Rd.   847/437-0300

Schaumburg Township
25 Illinois Blvd.
Hoffman Estates   847/884-0030

Parks and Recreation

Al Hattendorf Center
225 E. Elk Grove Blvd.   847/364-7224

Elk Grove Village Park District
499 Biesterfield Rd.   847/437-9494

The Farm House Museum
499 Biesterfield Rd.   847/439-3994

The Pavilion
1000 Wellington Ave.   847/437-9494

Pirates Cove Theme Park
Biesterfield and Leicester roads   847/439-2683

Teen Center
Lions Park Community Center
180 Morrison Dr.   847/437-4220

Libraries

Elk Grove Village Public Library
1001 Wellington Ave.   847/439-0447

Schools

School Districts

Community Consolidated School District 54
524 E. Schaumburg Rd.
Schaumburg   847/885-6700

Community Consolidated School District 59
2123 S. Arlington Heights Rd.   847/593-4300

Community High School District 211
1750 S. Roselle Rd.
Palatine   847/359-3300

Community High School District 214
2121 S. Goebbert Rd.
Arlington Heights   847/718-7645

Community Colleges

Harper College
1200 W. Algonquin Rd.
Palatine   847/925-6000

Roosevelt University
Albert A. Robin Campus
1400 N. Roosevelt Blvd.
Schaumburg   847/619-8600

Selected Community Organizations

Community Service Department   847/357-4120

YES (Youth Employment Service)   847/357-4120

Houses of Worship

Calvary Chapel
1000 Wellington Ave.   847/895-3545

Christus Victor Lutheran Church
1045 S. Arlington Heights Rd.   847/437-2666

Elk Grove Baptist Church
801 Beisner Rd.   847/593-8337

Elk Grove Presbyterian Church
600 E. Elk Grove Blvd.   847/437-0770

First Baptist Church and Korean First Baptist Church
590 Tonne Rd.   847/427-1559

Gethsemane Presbyterian Church
301 Ridge Ave.   847/228-0008

Lutheran Church of the Holy Spirit
150 Lions Dr.   847/437-5897

Prince of Peace United Methodist Church
1400 S. Arlington Heights Rd.   847/439-0668

Queen of the Rosary Church
750 W. Elk Grove Blvd.   847/437-0403

St. Julian Church
601 Biesterfield Rd.   847/956-0130

St. Nicholas Episcopal Church
1072 Ridge Ave.   847/439-2067

Wesleyan Community Church
545 Landmeier Rd.   847/437-8188

Word of Life Church
1231 E. Higgins Rd.   630/682-4710

DINING

Native's Choices

Villa Marcella
1115 Rohlwing Rd.
847/534-9700
Dining selections are somewhat scant in the village, but places like
Villa Marcella seek to correct that shortcoming. White tablecloths
and subdued lighting give the interior an intimate feel; an excellent
wine list and higher-end Italian cuisine round out the experience.
Open Mon. - Sat. 11 a.m. - 10 p.m. Closed Sun.

Autumn House Restaurant
1951 Busse Rd.
847/952-1119
One of the village's longest-running restaurants keeps locals coming back, often several times a week. The food is good (basic American), service is friendly and prompt, and prices are easy to swallow. Entrees from $10.95 to $19.95.
Open Mon. - Sat. 5:30 a.m. - 10 p.m., Sun. 5:30 a.m. - 8 p.m.

Espresso Brewery Company II
958 Elk Grove Town Center
847/718-9272
This is a particularly welcome addition to the area's nightlife because there just aren't many places like it. If you're looking for coffee or tea and a light dessert along with a helping of quality jazz, this is the place to be.
Open Mon. - Thurs. 6 a.m. - 10 p.m., Fri. 6 a.m. - 12 a.m., Sat. 8 a.m. - 12 a.m., Sun. 8 a.m. - 8 p.m.

Lou Malnati's Pizzeria
1050 E. Higgins Rd., 847/439-2000
85 S. Buffalo Grove Rd., Buffalo Grove, 847/215-7100
1 S. Roselle Rd., Schaumburg, 847/985-1525
This is a small, local chain that features great deep-dish pizza and heaping plates of Italian fare in a sports club atmosphere. Prices are average, about $8.95 to $16.95, and service is generally good, although crowds get thick at peak times.
Open Mon. - Sat. 11 a.m. - 11 p.m., Sun. 12 p.m. - 11 p.m.

ROSEMONT

Rosemont at a Glance

Incorporated: 1956
Population: 3,954
Median Household Income: $70,670
Median Home Value: $204,688

The term "shoo-in" must have been invented for Donald E. Stephens, who has reigned as the mayor of Rosemont since the village was established in 1954. There's no disputing his effectiveness; during his tenure the town has grown from a nameless plot of land to a sort of convention central for the Chicago region. Today, the downtown contains one of virtually every top-name hotel, has two major convention/conference centers and two large event venues, and hosts more than 25,000 visitors daily.

Most of those folks are just passing through, of course, but they keep the restaurants and bars pretty busy on any given night of the week.

The roughly 4,300 residents have to cope with the congestion of major thoroughfares, along with jet noise from the adjacent O'Hare International Airport. But they have the unique distinction of living in the community that is home to the Donald E. Stephens Museum of Hummels (see p. 108), housing more than 1,000 rare M.I. Hummels ceramic figurines and ANRI woodcarvings.

The Rosemont Horizon and Rosemont Theater (see p. 107) are the only major concert venues in the Northwest Suburbs, offering a full range of artists and shows. The Horizon is also home to the Chicago Wolves hockey team, which won the IHL championship in 1997, and the DePaul Blue Demons college basketball team.

If you need a nice place to work out, the Willow Creek Club offers a range of contemporary exercise equipment and classes, but more important, it also offers massage therapy, a steam room, sauna, and whirlpool. The facility is among the finest you'll find anywhere and almost makes working out a pleasure.

ESSENTIAL CONTACTS

Basics

Village Hall
9501 W. Devon Ave.   847/825-4404

Rosemont Convention Bureau
9301 W. Bryn Mawr Ave.   847/823-2100
The convention bureau serves as "information central" for the village,
offering connections to ten nearby hotels, as well as public information
and visitors guides.

Rosemont Convention Center
5555 N. River Rd.   847/823-2100

Rosemont Exposition Services
9301 W. Bryn Mawr Ave.   847/696-2208

Rosemont Department of Public Safety
Police and Fire (non-emergency)
9501 W. Devon Ave.   847/823-1134

Police, Fire, and Ambulance (emergency)   911

Townships

Maine Township
1700 Ballard Rd.
Park Ridge   847/297-2510

Parks and Recreation

Rosemont Park District
Margaret J. Lange Park
6140 Scott St.   847/823-6685

Schools

School Districts

Des Plaines School District 62
777 Algonquin Rd.
Des Plaines   847/824-1136

Leyden Community District 212
3400 Rose St.
Franklin Park   847/451-3000

Rosemont Elementary School District 78
6101 N. Ruby St.   847/825-0144

Houses of Worship

Our Lady of Hope
9711 W. Devon Ave.   847/825-4673

SITES

Rosemont Horizon
6920 N. Mannheim Rd.
847/635-6601
847/827-9696 (Chicago Wolves)
847/733-7700 (Wolves tickets)
Home of the Chicago Wolves IHL hockey team and DePaul Blue
Demons basketball and site of many concerts and sporting events
throughout the year, the Rosemont Horizon holds approximately
18,000 people.
*The Rosemont Horizon has just been sold to Allstate and will soon
undergo a name change. Everything else will remain the same.*

Rosemont Theater
5400 N. River Rd.
847/671-5100
Opened in 1995, the Rosemont Theater is the newest concert venue in

the suburbs and features excellent acoustics in a relatively intimate atmosphere. About 4,300 seats.

Donald E. Stephens Museum of Hummels
555 N. River Rd.
847/692-4000
In addition to being one of the longest-seated mayors in history, Rosemont leader Donald E. Stephens is an avid collector of M.I. Hummel figurines.

Willow Creek Club
10225 W. Higgins Rd.
847/698-2582
A complete fitness center, Willow Creek Club's facilities include a swimming pool, racquetball courts, exercise equipment, and classes. *Open to all with daily fees.*

DINING

Native's Choices

Carlucci Rosemont
6111 N. River Rd.
847/518-0990
The Carlucci family is well-known in the Chicago area; just about each sibling has a restaurant in one town or another. This is one of their best, featuring country Italian cuisine with modest beginnings but elegant execution. The open kitchen and roomy interior makes for a pleasant atmosphere, even when it's full, which it often is. Entrees $12-$20. *Open for lunch Mon. - Thurs. 11:30 a.m. - 2:30 p.m.; for dinner Mon. - Thurs. 5 p.m. - 10 p.m., Fri. - Sat. 5 p.m. - 11 p.m., Sun. 4:30 p.m. - 10 p.m.*

Morton's of Chicago/Rosemont
9525 W. Bryn Mawr Ave.
847/678-5155
There's no need to go into the city for an exceptional Chicago steak. This upscale restaurant is a real treat, and although prices are high ($15 to $30 per entree), the service, quality of food, and indulgent

atmosphere will guarantee a return visit. If you have business associates you want to impress, this is the place.

Open Mon. - Sat. 5 p.m. - 11 p.m., Sun. 5 p.m. - 10 p.m.

Nick's Fishmarket
10275 W. Higgins Rd. (at Mannheim Rd.)
847/298-8200

If your business clients like seafood, there are only two places to take them. (See also Bob Chinn's Crabhouse in *Wheeling,* p. 64.) Abalone may be the best bet on the menu, although you won't go wrong with lobster or crab legs. Nick's also offers a large bar popular with the after-work crowd. Live music and dancing offered on weekends. About $15 to $30 per entree.

Open Mon. - Thurs. 5:30 p.m. - 10 p.m., Fri. - Sat. 5:30 p.m. - 11 p.m., Sun. 5:30 p.m. - 9 p.m.

Worth Noting

Rib's Restaurant
9501 W. Devon Ave.
847/318-7591

Probably the most affordable of all of Rosemont's restaurants, Rib's features exactly what you might expect—baby backs smothered in tangy sauce. The substantial, dinner-sized salads are also worth a try; otherwise, the sandwiches and standard American fare is good, but uninspired. Entrees range from about $6 to $17.

Open Mon. - Thurs. 11:30 a.m. - 10 p.m., Fri. - Sat. 11:30 a.m. - 11 p.m., with downstairs bar open Mon. - Sat. until 4 a.m. Closed Sun.

Rosewood
9421 W. Higgins Rd.
847/696-9494

Try to get a seat near the fireplace and prepare for a long, comfortable evening. The fare is strictly American, but there are some nice influences from other cultures that sneak on to the menu. Entrees range from about $10 to $25.

Open for lunch Mon. - Fri. 11 a.m. - 3:45 p.m., for dinner daily 4 p.m. - 10:30 p.m.

ENTERTAINMENT

Hotel Hot-Spots

Just about every bar and restaurant in Rosemont, other than those mentioned above, is located in one of the dozen or so hotels that serve as the social hub of the city. Of the following, you'll find the most locals at Shoeless Joe's, especially when WSCR-AM sports radio talk show hosts, Mike North and Dan Jiggetts, broadcast their show there (they also have shows at Carlucci occasionally).

At the Hop
Holiday Inn-O'Hare International
5440 N. River Rd.   847/671-6350

The Bar
Rosemont Suites Hotel O'Hare
5500 N. River Rd.   888/476-7366

The Kona Kai
The O'Hare Marriott
8535 W. Higgins Rd.   773/693-4444

Le Bar
Hotel Sofitel
5550 N. River Rd.   847/678-4488

Maxie's
Clarion International/Quality Inn at O'Hare
6810 N. Mannheim Rd.   847/297-1234

New Image Sport Bar
Hyatt Regency O'Hare
9300 W. Bryn Mawr Ave.   847/696-1234

The Quest Sports Bar
Ramada Plaza Hotel O'Hare
6600 N. Mannheim Rd.   847/827-5131

72 West
Sheraton Gateway Suites O'Hare
6501 N. Mannheim Rd.   847/699-6300

Shoeless Joe's
Best Western at O'Hare
10300 W. Higgins Rd.   847/296-4471

Teddy Rose
The Westin O'Hare
6100 N. River Rd.   847/698-6000

LAKE ZURICH, KILDEER, HAWTHORN WOODS, WAUCONDA, AND ISLAND LAKE

The view of Bangs Lake from the Biloxi Grill in Wauconda.

Island Lake, Wauconda, and Lake Zurich

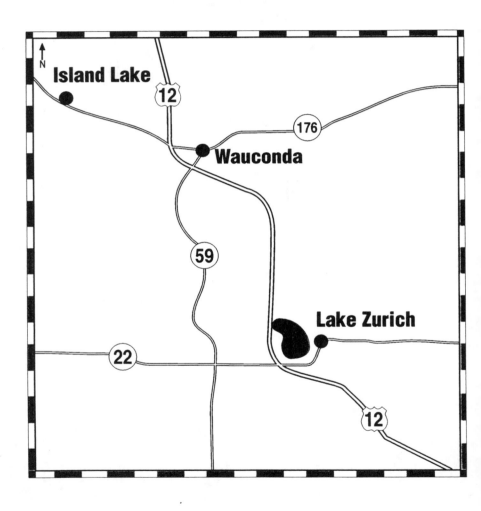

LAKE ZURICH, KILDEER, AND HAWTHORN WOODS

Lake Zurich at a Glance

Incorporated: 1896
Population: 16,786
Median Household Income: $90,680
Median Home Value: $230,647

The area known as Lake Zurich was first settled by George Ela in 1835. At that time, the small lake that now serves as the recreational focal point of the village was called Cedar Lake, and when Ela became the township's first postmaster, the village was called Surryse.

Seth Paine also settled in the village around that time and is credited with building the first major structures in town. His contributions of a general store, a saw mill, and a meeting hall (which also served as a school and later, a stop along the underground railroad) gave the village its first commercial foundation.

On September 19, 1896, the village was officially incorporated as Lake Zurich and was settled mostly by German immigrants and New England farmers.

By the 1950s, Lake Zurich, along with the nearby villages of Wauconda and Island Lake, had become a summer resort town for Chicagoans. Some of that character remains, along Main Street at least, in the architecture and layout of buildings surrounding the lake.

Downtown Lake Zurich is charming, a bit old-fashioned, and friendly. Village leaders are considering some changes that would make the businesses in this area slightly more accessible to visitors, as parking spaces are at a premium.

The area immediately surrounding Lake Zurich has become home to the suburban bane of strip malls. A two-mile stretch along Route 12 (Rand Road) features the usual collection of grocery stores, retail shops, and fast-food restaurants, although a handful of dining establishments stand out from the rest.

kildeer at a Glance
Incorporated: 1958
Population: 2,821
Median Household Income: $208,547
Median Home Value: $500,000

Hawthorn Woods at a Glance
Incorporated: 1958
Population: 5,498
Median Household Income: $135,923
Median Home Value: $445,485

In 1958, Kildeer and Hawthorn Woods were literally established as defenses against encroaching development, an attitude that continues to define the area. Both villages today are primarily bedroom communities with about 2,500 and 5,000 residents, respectively, and independent village governments. The average cost of a home in either town approaches $500,000.

Kemper Insurance Co. is the primary corporate presence in the area; the golf course that lies on the sprawling property along Route 22 is the site of an annual professional golf tournament. The course is stellar if you can afford it: green fees exceed $100.

ESSENTIAL CONTACTS

Basics

Lake Zurich Village Hall
70 E. Main St.   847/438-5141

Lake Zurich Area Chamber of Commerce
One NBD Plaza
Lake Zurich   847/438-5572

Police (non-emergency)   847/438-2349

Fire (non-emergency)   847/540-5070

Lake Zurich Rural Fire Protection District (non-emergency)
(includes most of Kildeer)   847/438-2349

Paramedics (non-emergency)   847/540-5070

Police, Fire, and Ambulance (emergency)   911

Village of Hawthorn Woods
2 Lagoon Dr.
Hawthorn Woods   847/438-5500

Police Department (non-emergency)
2 Lagoon Dr.
Hawthorn Woods   847/438-9050

Fire Department (non-emergency)   847/526-2821

Police, Fire, and Ambulance (emergency)   911

Village of Kildeer
22049 Chestnut Ridge   847/438-6000

Police (non-emergency)   847/438-6010

Police, Fire, and Ambulance (emergency)   911

Long Grove Rural Fire Protection District
(includes eastern portion of Kildeer)
Non-Emergency   847/634-3143
Emergency   847/634-3141

Townships

Ela Township
95 E. Main St.   847/438-7823

Parks and Recreation

Hawthorn Woods Parks and Recreation
2 Lagoon Dr.
Hawthorn Woods   847/438-5520

Lake Zurich Parks and Recreation
Paulus Park
400 Whitney Rd.   847/438-5146

Libraries

Ela Area Public Library
135 S. Buesching Rd.   847/438-3433

Schools

School Districts

Elementary School District 96
777 Checker Dr.
Buffalo Grove   847/459-4260

Lake Zurich District 95
400 S. Old Rand Rd.   847/438-2831

Stevenson High School District 125
1 Stevenson Dr.
Lincolnshire   847/634-4000

Selected Community Organizations

Cultural Arts Connection
(Ela Festival of the Arts)   847/289-4343

Ela Historical Society
95 E. Main St.   847/438-6490

Ela Township Seniors   847/438-0303

Garden Club of Lake Zurich   847/382-2621

Hawthorn Woods Women's Club   847/726-7713

Lake Zurich Playhouse   847/540-5932

Omni Youth Services
1616 N. Arlington Heights Rd.   847/253-6010
Arlington Heights

Welcome Wagon/Newcomers' Club   847/540-6123

DINING

Native's Choices

Fritzl's European Inn
900 Ravinia Terr.
847/540-8844
Exceptional preparation and presentation mark this restaurant known throughout the area for its authentic German cuisine. Prices are a little higher than average ($12.95-$25.95), but worth it.
Open Tues. - Sat. 4 p.m. - around 10 p.m., Sun. 12 p.m. - around 9 p.m. Closed Mon.

Hackney's Restaurant
880 N. Old Rand Rd.
847/438-2103
If you want a great hamburger, there's no reason to look anywhere else. Hackney's also features an extensive selection of classic American fare; don't miss the onion loaf appetizer, but order a half-size for two or less. A local favorite.
Open Mon. - Thurs. 11:15 a.m. - 11 p.m., Fri. - Sat. 11 a.m. - 12 a.m., Sun. 11:45 a.m. - 11 p.m.

Julio's Latin Cafe
99 S. Rand Rd.
847/438-3484
Julio's is one of my three favorite places. Its Latin American cuisine ranging from flavorful *ceviche* to enormous *paellas* make this bright, pleasant restaurant a joy to experience. Service is excellent, and prices at $9.95 to $16.95 are quite affordable. Be sure to try one of the dozens of sipping tequilas available, and don't skip the banana dessert.
Open for lunch Mon. - Fri. 11:30 a.m. - 2:30 p.m.; for dinner Mon. - Thurs. 5 p.m. - 9 p.m., Fri. - Sat. 5 p.m. - 10 p.m., Sun. 4:30 p.m. - 8:30 p.m.

Worth Noting

Brother's Ribs
69 S. Rand Rd.
847/540-7427
Brother's ribs consistently win nods for outstanding barbecue sauce and tender meat. Prices are low ($6.95-$15), service is fast, and the nice take-out packaging keeps everything warm for your picnic at Paulus Park on Lake Zurich.
Open Mon. - Thurs. 4 p.m. - 9 p.m., Fri. - Sat. 11:30 a.m. - 10 p.m., Sun. 1 p.m. - 9 p.m.

Eng's Tea House
710 N. Old Rand Rd.
847/438-6401
On the north "coast" of Lake Zurich, this humble little Cantonese restaurant is a diamond in the rough. Entrees are very inexpensive

(little is more than $10) and the staff is friendly and helpful; just try to ignore the modest décor of red-checked vinyl tablecloths and kitschy wall hangings.

Open Tues. - Thurs. 11 a.m. - 9 p.m., Fri. 11 a.m. - 10 p.m., Sat. 12 p.m. - 10 p.m., Sun. 12 p.m. - 9 p.m. Closed Mon.

D&J Bistro
466 S. Rand Rd.
847/438-8001
D&J Bistro is a disarmingly casual bistro that brings locals back time after time. The fixed-price, three-course option is a great choice at $24 per person; otherwise expect to spend about $30 per person, with a glass of wine.

Open for lunch Tues. - Fri. 11:30 a.m. - 2:30 p.m.; for dinner Tues. - Sat. 5 p.m. - 9:30 p.m., Sun. 4:30 p.m. - 9 p.m.

JJ Twigs Pizza & Pub
173 W. Main St.
847/438-5800
This friendly neighborhood pub is about as casual as you can get, but locals swear by the prices and the pizza. Almost always a crowd on weekends.

Opens daily at 11 a.m. Closing varies but is usually around 12 a.m., later on weekends.

Taylor Street Steakhouse
235 S. Rand Rd.
847/438-4499
A long-time favorite of suburbanites, the restaurant seemed to fizzle a bit a year or so ago. Now in a new location, they've revitalized both the menu and the kitchen, adding top-quality steaks to an otherwise Italian-inspired menu. Prices fall in the $14.95 to $24.95 range, though some large combo platters top the $35 mark.

Open for lunch Mon. - Fri. 11 a.m. - 3 p.m.; for dinner Mon. - Thurs. 4:30 p.m. - 10 p.m., Fri. - Sat. 4:30 p.m. - 11 p.m., Sun. 4 p.m. - 9 p.m.

Stonegate Tavern
500 Ela Rd.
847/438-4900
A popular place for the business-lunch and after-work crowd, Stonegate has managed to maintain an excellent and well-priced menu of mostly American classics, along with a few types of fish and pasta.

Dinner prices range from $9.95 to $18.95; lunches are a few dollars cheaper.

Open Mon. - Sat. 11 a.m. - 12 a.m., Sun. 11 a.m. - 9 p.m.

WAUCONDA AND ISLAND LAKE

Wauconda at a Glance

Incorporated: 1877
Population: 8,461
Median Household Income: $56,504
Median Home Value: $140,700

Driving along any of the busy Northwest Suburban byways, it's hard to imagine that once upon a time places like Wauconda, Island Lake, and Lake Zurich were considered far enough away from Chicago to be vacation destinations for urban dwellers.

But there was a time when these "resort communities" flourished simply for the fact that they were both remote and beautiful. The focus of each town is a large, lovely lake edged by beaches, stocked with fish, and filled with leisure boats as soon as the weather turns warm.

The northwoods cabin-style structures bordering Bangs Lake in Wauconda are a reminder of a time when Chicago suburbs were rural. But they also serve, in a way, to preserve that image—one cherished by most of the people who live here.

Life seems to pass just a little bit more slowly in Wauconda and Island Lake; people seem to be just a little bit friendlier, and churches are mostly full on Sunday mornings.

That Wauconda is a Christian community is unmistakable. In the early 1990s, atheist activist Rob Sherman, a Buffalo Grove resident, successfully protested the fact that religious images were being displayed on government-owned property. Those were removed, but almost overnight, hundreds of crosses appeared on lawns and buildings throughout the village; most of them remain in place.

Against the village's rural backdrop is the almost constant sound of hammers as new housing developments appear. Housing prices, in general, are slightly more affordable in this neck of the woods, ranging from about $130,000 to $260,000, with a handful breaking the $300,000 mark.

Large businesses have long made their home in Wauconda. Among the most notable is Chicago Cutlery, makers of fine knives for personal and professional kitchens.

The fact that Wauconda rests at the junction of routes 12, 59, and 173 makes it slightly easier to get to (and therefor slightly more populated) than Island Lake. That has allowed more of Island Lake's rural past to survive, even in the face of continuing growth and development in what is arguably the farthest corner of what we call the Northwest Suburbs.

Island Lake at a Glance

Incorporated: 1952
Population: 7,464
Median Household Income: $55,303
Median Home Value: $140,100

Island Lake has the dubious distinction of having made tabloid headlines in the early 1990s. A story in the *National Enquirer* claimed a lake monster lived in the depths of the village's namesake body of water, threatening to consume everything from fish to young children.

The story gave everyone a good laugh, in spite of the fact that in some ways, the truth was much stranger. The lake had become home to a particular breed of snapping turtle, one of which was rumored to have been hungry enough to attack a small dog.

As a news editor at the time, my staff and I were never able to confirm that part of the story. But the event, as a whole, left me with a fondness for the community and its leaders that has remained to this day.

ESSENTIAL CONTACTS

Basics

Wauconda Village Hall
101 N. Main St.   847/526-9600

Wauconda Chamber of Commerce
213 S. Main St.   847/526-5580

Wauconda Police Department
311 S. Main St. (Old Rand Rd.)   847/526-2421

Wauconda Fire Department (Main Station)
109 W. Liberty St.   847/526-2821

Island Lake Village Hall
3720 Greenleaf Ave.   847/526-8764

Island Lake Chamber of Commerce
227 W. State Rd.   847/487-4522

Island Lake Police Department
3720 Greenleaf Ave.   847/526-2100

Fire Department
A branch station of the Wauconda Fire Department serves Island Lake.
See Wauconda Fire Department listing above.

Townships

Vernon Township
3050 N. Main St.
Prairie View   847/634-4600

Wauconda Township
505 Bonner Rd.
Wauconda   847/526-2631

Parks and Recreation

Island Lake Recreation Department
3720 Greenleaf Ave.   847/526-4851

Wauconda Park District
600 N. Main St.   847/526-3610

Libraries

Wauconda Area Public Library
801 N. Main St.   847/526-6225

Schools

School Districts

Wauconda Community School District 118
555 N. Main St.   847/526-7690

Houses of Worship

Church of the Holy Apostles
26238 N. Rt. 59   847/526-7148

Evangelical Free Church
27215 N. Anderson Rd.   847/526-8254

Federated Church of Wauconda
200 Barrington Rd.   847/526-8471

Iglesia Evangelica Libre
27215 N. Anderson Rd.   847/526-5629

Messiah Lutheran Church
25225 W. Ivanhoe Rd.   847/526-7161

Roberts Road Baptist Church
290902 W. Roberts (at Darrell Rd.)
Island Lake   847/639-2419

St. John Lutheran Church
Rt. 176
Island Lake   847/526-7614

Transfiguration Church
318 Bangs St.   847/526-2400

DINING

Native's Choices

The Biloxi Grill
313 E. Liberty St.
847/526-2420
David and Catherine Koelling may be the prototype for the new
suburban restaurateur. Their restaurant could easily hold up against
any competition in the city, but they've opted instead to bring their
inventiveness to the suburbs.

Having operated the successful, somewhat upscale Greenery restaurant
in Barrington until two years ago, the Koellings decided to try something new.

Drawing on their training with the famed Brennan family at the presti-
gious Commander's Palace in New Orleans, they opened the Biloxi
Grill, offering a wide range of creative entrees with a Southern flair.

A visit to the Biloxi Grill is notable first for Catherine's buoyant charm
and personality. You are made to feel equally welcome whether visiting the rustic bar or the simple, comfortable dining room, either of
which offer a tremendous view of Wauconda's Bangs Lake.

What Catherine does for the front of the house, David equals in the
kitchen. A typical meal might include the crab cake appetizer, the
"soup sipper"—a hearty sampling of the four soups of the day, and

one of the many entrees ranging from Creole grilled shrimp to jamba-laya, Black Angus steak, or smoked duck.

The mostly American wine list is carefully selected, and the wait staff is thoroughly versed on all of the selections; try the Cakebread reserve Chardonnay.

Live jazz is offered in the bar on Thursday nights, and a small but enthusiastic Southern folk/rock band takes over on Fridays after 7 p.m. The bar is well-stocked and includes a small selection of microbrews and cigars. A late-night bar menu is also available.

If all of that doesn't convince you, the attitude expressed in the restaurant philosophy should: "Sit back, eat much, laugh often."
Open Tues. - Sun. 11:30 a.m. - 10 p.m.

Main Street Café
122 S. Main St.
847/526-9256
If you're looking for a good, hearty breakfast, the Main Street Café is the place to visit. Prices are cheap, people are friendly, and the chef even gets creative from time to time. So creative, in fact, that they decided to open for dinner three nights a week,Wednesday through Friday.
Open Mon. - Tues. 7 a.m. - 2 p.m., Wed. - Fri. 7 a.m. - 9 p.m., Sat. - Sun. 7 a.m. - 1 p.m.

O'Traina's Lakeside Eatery & Tavern
110 S. Main St.
847/26-4499
The restaurant is to the left as you walk in, the tavern is on the right. Both are great places to spend time. The bar is filled with friendly locals, and they occasionally feature live music. The restaurant offers excellent fare that almost makes the term "eatery" misleading. Prices range from $9.95 to $15.95.
Open Tues. - Thurs. 11 a.m. - 11 p.m., Fri. - Sat. 11 a.m. - 2 a.m., Sun. 11 a.m. - 10 p.m. Closing hours vary depending on the crowd.

Spasso
614 W. Liberty St.
847/26-4215
It seems out-of-the-way, and perhaps even out of place, but make no

mistake, Spasso is one of the absolute finest Italian restaurants around. They somehow manage to combine a casual atmosphere with *nouveau* accents without charging an arm and a leg. Price range from $11.95 to $19.95.

Open for lunch Mon. - Fri. 11:30 a.m. - 2:30 p.m., dinner served Mon.- Thurs. 5 p.m. - 9:30 p.m., Fri. - Sat. 5 p.m. - 10:30 p.m., Sun. 4 p.m. - 9 p.m.

Worth Noting

Bonner Road Inn

722 E. Bonner Rd.

Wauconda

847/26-8550

The Bonner Road Inn is one of those friendly little out-of-the-way places that you love to come across on day drives and road trips. There's something of the Wisconsin north woods in the interior; the menu is above average tavern fare mostly priced below $10.

Open daily 10 a.m. - 2 a.m. Closing hours vary depending on the crowd.

Island Lake Inn Restaurant

310 E. State Rd.

Island Lake

847/526-7797

A very popular choice among locals looking for good American food with a smattering of international influences thrown in. Prices are reasonable, mostly falling between $8 and $15 (breakfast is much less). Like almost every restaurant in Wauconda and Island Lake, the staff and the patrons both make you feel like you're a regular the moment you walk in the door.

Open Mon. - Sat. 6 a.m. - 10 p.m., Sun. 6 a.m - 9 p.m.

Muncione's Pizzeria Restaurant

206 E. State Rd.

Island Lake

847/526-8700

Muncione's is a long-standing favorite in the village. The staff treats you like a regular even if you aren't, and the prices are very affordable. I've honestly never had a bad meal here—the pizza's are the hottest

thing on the menu (take-out or dine in) for good reason.
Open Sun. - Thurs. 11 a.m. - 10 p.m., Fri. - Sat. 11 a.m. - 11 p.m.

PALATINE
AND
ROLLING
MEADOWS

Community Church in Rolling Meadows.

Palatine, Rolling Meadows, and Arlington Heights

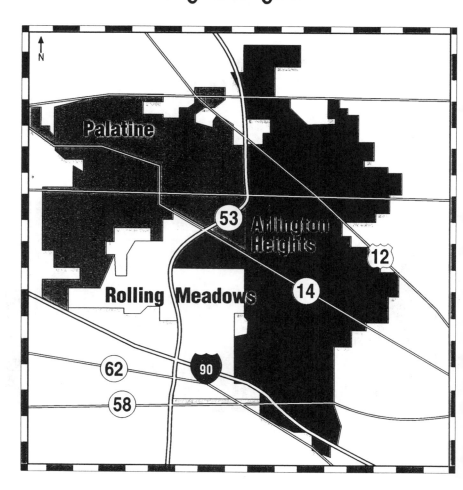

PALATINE

Palatine at a Glance

Incorporated: 1866
Population: 44,460
Median Household Income: $72,390
Median Home Value: $201,535

Like its southern neighbor, Schaumburg, Palatine's history is marked by substantial population growth since the 1960s. That left village leaders with a number of challenges, not least of which was to preserve some sense of a village center. They largely succeeded in the downtown area near the train station, where restaurants and nightclubs (Mia Cucina, Durty Nellie's) keep people around well into the night.

Affordable housing for both renters and home buyers and easy access from major highways and public transportation also inflated the population of Township High School 211, the largest high school district in Illinois. Five high schools, with a combined enrollment of more than 11,500, are located within the boundaries of 211.

Education seems to be the thing in Palatine. William Rainey Harper College, recognized as one of the top community colleges in the nation, makes its home on the north end of the village.

Among Palatine's corporate claims to fame are the Weber Grill Company (not the restaurant, the actual place they make the things) and the international headquarters of Square D.

ESSENTIAL CONTACTS

Basics

Village of Palatine
200 E. Wood St.   847/358-7500

Greater Palatine Chamber of Commerce & Industry
652 N. North Ct., Ste. 100   847/359-7200

Police Department (non-emergency)
200 E. Wood St.   847/359-9000

Fire Department (non-emergency)
Station 18 (administration headquarters)
39 E. Colfax St.   847/202-6340

Fire Prevention Division
200 E. Wood St.   847/359-9029

Police, Fire, and Ambulance (emergency)   911

Townships

Palatine Township
721 S. Quentin Rd.   847/358-6700

Parks and Recreation

Palatine Park District
250 E. Wood St.   847/991-0333

Salt Creek Park District
530 S. Williams Ave.   847/259-6890

Libraries

Freeman Road Branch
1262 Freeman Rd.
Hoffman Estates   847/934-0220

Palatine Public Library
700 N. North Ct.   847/358-5881

Schools

School Districts

High School District 211
G.A. McElroy Administrative Center   847/755-6600

Palatine Community Consolidated School District 15
580 N. First Bank Dr.   847/963-3032

Private Elementary Schools

St. Colette School
3900 Pheasant Dr.
Rolling Meadows   847/392-4098

St. Thomas of Villanova School
1141 E. Anderson Dr.   847/358-2110

Community College

Harper College
1200 W. Algonquin Rd.   847/925-6000
www.harper.cc.il.us
Harper College serves 23 communities around and including Palatine.

Selected Community Organizations

Home of the Sparrow
1509 Oak St.   847/963-8030

Newcomers Club of Palatine
223 E. Parallel St.   847/358-8757

Northern Illinois Business Association
625 N. North Ct., Ste. 300   847/963-9860

Palatine Business & Professional Women
749 N. Williams Ave.   847/776-0499

Palatine Township Senior Citizens Council
505 S. Quentin Rd.   847/991-1112

Palatine Women's Club
P.O. Box 1822   847/358-1147

Houses of Worship

All Saints Lutheran Church
630 S. Quentin Rd.   847/991-2080

Christ Lutheran Church
41 S. Rohlwing Rd.   847/358-4600

Deer Grove Covenant Church
345 N. Quentin Rd.   847/202-0930

First Baptist Church of Palatine
1023 E. Palatine Rd.   847/358-4224

First United Methodist Church of Palatine
123 N. Plum Grove Rd.   847/359-1345

Grace Community Church
579 First Bank Dr.   847/776-1900

Immaculate Conception Ukrainian Catholic Church
745 S. Benton St.   847/991-0820

Immanuel Lutheran Church
200 N. Plum Grove Rd.   847/359-1549

Prince of Peace Lutheran Church
1190 N. Hicks Rd.   847/359-3451

St. Nectarios Greek Orthodox Church
133 S. Roselle Rd.   847/358-5170

St. Paul United Church of Christ
144 E. Palatine Rd.   847/358-0399

St. Theresa Church
467 N. Benton St.   847/358-7760

DINING

Native's Choices

Burning Ambitions Smoke Shop and Cigar Bar
19 N. Bothwell St.
847/358-0200
There's something a little indulgent about this place: it's like a country club without the club, or maybe just an after-hours hideaway that gives you an hour or so of vacation. At any rate, the food is excellent, as is the wine list and selection of cognacs and scotch ... oh, and of course, the cigars. An excellent ventilation system keeps the library-style décor from filling with smoke. Prices range from $7.95 (burgers) to $28.95 (12-oz prime New York sirloin).
Open Mon. - Thurs. 11 a.m. - 12 a.m., Fri. - Sat. 11 a.m. - 1 a.m. Closed Sun.

Carpaccio
2001 N. Rand Rd.
847/202-1191
This restaurant opened only a couple of years ago, but it quickly

jumped to the top of the pack in terms of fine Italian cuisine. Prices generally fall in the mid-teens, and dress is business casual. The intimate and cozy interior, along with a well-chosen wine list, makes it a great spot for a romantic evening.

Open for lunch Mon. - Fri. 11:30 a.m. - 2:30 p.m., for dinner daily 4:30 p.m. - 10 p.m.

Marlowe's
704 W. Euclid Ave.
847/991-7540
As high-toned as the interior seems, Marlowe's welcomes families. Good prices for good food keep mom and dad's budget safe, and while the menu is mostly American, nothing is missing. Any of Marlowe's steak or pork entrees are excellent choices.

Open Mon. - Thurs. 11:30 a.m. - 10 p.m., Fri. - Sat. 11:30 a.m. - 11 p.m., Sun. brunch 10 a.m. - 2 p.m. (lunch menu until 4 p.m.), Sun. dinner 4 p.m. - 9 p.m.

Worth Noting

Slice of Chicago
36 S. Northwest Hwy.
847/991-2150
The type of music varies at Slice of Chicago from Chicago blues to pop rock, but the acts are always quality. Good Italian and American food is available in front—the back is where the action is and where you'll pay a low cover (usually $5 or less) for the entertainment.

Open Sun. - Thurs. 11 a.m. - 3 a.m., Fri. - Sat. 11 a.m. - 4 a.m.

ROLLING MEADOWS

Rolling Meadows at a Glance

Incorporated: 1955
Population: 22,560
Median Household Income: $67,222
Median Home Value: $183,800

For a time, Rolling Meadows was kind of a reflection of neighboring Palatine and Arlington Heights. But lately that's all changed. With continuing efforts to beautify and simplify the downtown area, the personality of the city is really taking shape.

Of course, the city has always been blessed with the presence of some big players in the corporate world. Northrop Grumman and Pepsi both have large offices, and U.S. Robotics is building a complex as well.

Route 53 divides the community into two sides. The east side of the highway is the oldest, where the homes date back to the city's creation in 1953, when developer Kimball Hill envisioned a place with quality homes at reasonable prices.

Most single-family detached homes in Rolling Meadows now sell between $180,000 and $225,000, and the median household income here is about $70,000.

The city is fortunate to be home to one of the most active and successful arts organizations in the suburbs, the Northwest Cultural Council. In addition to an exceptional art gallery offering the works of 30 or more artists, the council also holds an annual writer's conference and offers poetry readings each month. It's well worth your time to visit this gallery. For directions and hours, call 847/956-7966.

ESSENTIAL CONTACTS

Basics

City Hall
3600 Kirchoff Rd. 847/394-8500

Rolling Meadows Chamber of Commerce
3600 Kirchoff Rd., Ste. 300 847/398-3730

Police Department (non-emergency)
3600 Kirchoff Rd. 847/255-2416

Fire Department (non-emergency)
2455 Plum Grove Rd. 847/397-3352

Police, Fire, and Ambulance (emergency) 911

Townships

Palatine Township
721 S. Quentin Rd.
Palatine 847/358-6700

Parks and Recreation

Community Center
Salt Park
3705 Pheasant Dr. 847/818-3200

Northrop Teen Center 847/818-3208

Rolling Meadows Park District
Administration
3000 Central Rd. 847/818-3220

Sports Complex
Salt Park
3705 Pheasant Dr. 847/818-3210

West Meadows Ice Arena
3900 Winnetka Ave.   847/398-2700

Libraries

Rolling Meadows Public Library
3110 Martin Ln.   847/259-6050

Schools

School Districts

High School District 211
G.A. McElroy Administrative Center   847/755-6600

Palatine Community Consolidated School District 15
580 N. First Bank Dr.
Palatine   847/963-3032

Township High School District 214
Forest View Educational Center
2121 S. Goebbert Rd.   847/718-7600

Private Elementary Schools

St. Colette Elementary School
3900 Pheasant Dr.   847/392-4098

Community Colleges

Harper College
1200 W. Algonquin Rd.
Palatine   847/925-6000

Houses of Worship

Beth Tikvah Congregation
300 Hillcrest Blvd.
Hoffman Estates   847/885-4545

Chinese Baptist Church of the Northwest Suburbs
4242 Kirchoff Rd.   847/934-4223

Church of Christ
2300 Cardinal Dr.   847/259-2995

Church of Jesus Christ of Latter-Day Saints
2035 N. Windsor Dr.
Arlington Heights   847/398-9662

Community Church of Rolling Meadows
2720 Kirchoff Rd.   847/255-5510

Cornerstone Church
3201 Meadow Dr.   847/818-1212

Harvest Bible Chapel
800 Rohlwing Rd.   847/398-7005

Iglesia Corona De Amor
800 Rohlwing Rd.   847/670-0304

Meadows Baptist Church
2401 Kirchoff Rd.   847/255-8764

St. Colette Catholic Church
3900 Meadow Dr.   847/394-8100

Trinity Lutheran Church
3201 Meadow Dr.   847/398-7122

ENTERTAINMENT

Opera in Focus
Rolling Meadows Park District Central
3000 Central Rd.
847/818-3220
Opera in Focus is a fascinating and entertaining celebration of opera
performed by exquisite, life-like puppets. The characters enact scenes
from the more popular operas; after the performance, the audience can

view the workings backstage and speak to the puppeteers. A must-see for children and adults.

Tickets are $9 for adults, $8 for seniors, and $6 for children. Reservations are required.

DINING

Native's Choices

Atrium
3223 W. Algonquin Rd.
847/259-7070
The long track record of this pleasant restaurant, which opened in 1974, says a lot for both the quality of food and the service. It's your basic selection of high-end American fare, from salmon to chateaubriand; the interior is romantic and spacious, perfect for impressing business execs or stealing away for an intimate rendezvous. Our choice: baby rack of lamb. Prices from about $15.95 to $21.95.
Open for lunch Mon. - Sat. 11 a.m. - 3 p.m.; for dinner Mon. - Thurs. 5 p.m. - 9 p.m., Fri. 5 p.m. - 10 p.m., Sat. 5 p.m. - 11 p.m., Sun. 4 p.m. - 9 p.m.; for brunch Sun. 10:30 a.m. - 3 p.m.

Rockhouse Grill
2212 Algonquin Rd.
847/392-6446
There are two faces to the Rockhouse Grill: one is the great restaurant, the other is the bar that serves as a great weekend venue for up-and-coming regional rock bands. Cover is usually $4 or less, and food prices aren't bad, either at $9.95 to $14.95.
Open Sun. - Thurs. 11 a.m. - 2 a.m., Fri. - Sat. 11 a.m. - 3:30 a.m.

Worth Noting

Rupert's for Steaks
1701 Golf Rd.
847/952-8555
Rupert's has been around for so long that it qualifies as an institution.

Tucked at the base of a large office complex, you can bet it draws a sizable after-work crowd of well-dressed business folks who generally stay for the fantastic steaks. Prices are average for a steakhouse, from around $10.95 to $21.95.

Open for lunch Mon. - Fri. 11 a.m. - 2 p.m.; for dinner Mon. - Fri. 5 p.m. - 10 p.m., Sat. 5 p.m. - 11 p.m. Closed Sun.

SCHAUMBURG, STREAMWOOD,
AND
HOFFMAN ESTATES

The winding pathways of Woodfield Mall in Schaumburg.

Hoffman Estates, Streamwood, Schaumburg, and Elk Grove Village

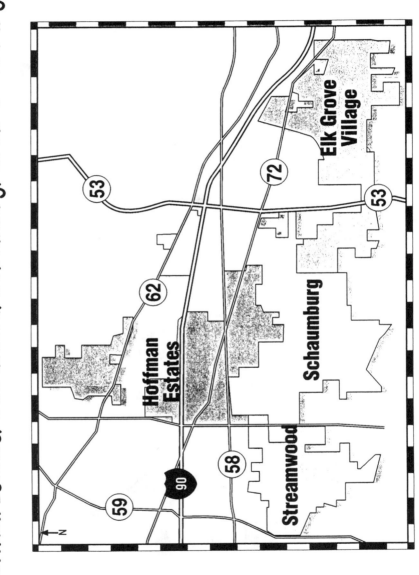

SCHAUMBURG

Schaumburg at a Glance

Incorporated: 1956
Population: 74,294
Median Household Income: $70,309
Median Home Value: $180,700

Historians in Schaumburg love to share the story of an 1850 township meeting at which landowner Frederick Nerge stood and said *"Schaumburg schall et heiten!"* ("Schaumburg it will be called"), after the Schaumburg-Lippe area of Germany from which he and many other area settlers had emigrated. Prior to that, the Schaumburg area was known as Sarah's Grove.

Though possibly apocryphal, the name stuck and Schaumburg became a popular farming community with a modest market area in what is now near the center of the village.

Officially incorporated in 1956, Schaumburg quickly became one of the largest of Chicago's suburbs. Like most of the Northwest Suburbs, the introduction of rail lines and stations created easy access to Chicago and almost directly paralleled significant population growth. The village is now host to several major corporations, a vast and thriving retail culture, and several satellite campuses of schools, including Roosevelt University, ITT Technical Institute, Lake Forest Graduate School of Management, and the Keller Graduate School of Management.

Motorola built its corporate headquarters there in 1968 and now employs more than 7,000 people; Woodfield Mall opened in 1971. Other companies based in Schaumburg include Zurich-American Insurance, Signature Group, Cellular One, Pioneer Financial Services, Xerox, and Texas Instruments, and IKEA, an enormous and highly visible furniture store. It's the big blue and yellow building near I-90 and Route 53.

Today, more than 74,000 people call Schaumburg home, where the median home value is around $180,000, and household incomes hover between $60,000 and $80,000.

While Schaumburg has recently made significant strides in creating a town square, the heart of the village will probably always be Woodfield Mall. It now ranks fourth in the U.S. in terms of size at almost three million square feet and during the holiday season can draw more than 150,000 people a day.

Many of the restaurants, particularly in the immediate vicinity of the mall, are chains geared toward mall and office employees. You'll find the same crowd at the local nightclubs as well.

ESSENTIAL CONTACTS

Basics

Schaumburg Village Hall
101 Schaumburg Ct.   847/895-4500

Greater Woodfield Convention and Visitors Bureau
1375 E. Woodfield Rd., Ste. 100   847/605-1010

Police Department (non-emergency)
1000 W. Schaumburg Rd.   847/882-3586

Fire Department (non-emergency)
1601 N. Roselle Rd.   847/885-6300

Police, Fire, and Ambulance (emergency)   911

Townships

Hanover Township
8N180 IL Rt. 59
Bartlett   630/837-0301

Palatine Township
721 S. Quentin Rd.
Palatine   847/358-6700

Schaumburg Township
25 Illinois Blvd.
Hoffman Estates   847/884-0030

Parks and Recreation

Schaumburg Park District
235 Beach St.   847/490-7015

Schaumburg Prairie Center for the Arts
201 Schaumburg Ct.   847/895-3600

Spring Valley Nature Center
1111 E. Schaumburg Rd.   847/985-2100

Water Works Aquatic Center
505 N. Springinsguth Rd.   847/490-7020

Libraries

Hanover Park branch
1570 Irving Park Rd.
Hanover Park   630/372-7800

Hoffman Estates branch
1890 Hassell Rd. (in Village Hall)
Hoffman Estates   847/885-3511

Schaumburg Township District Library
130 S. Roselle Rd.   847/985-4000

Schools

School Districts

Elgin School District U46
355 E. Chicago St.
Elgin   847/888-5000

Palatine Community Consolidated School District 15
580 N. First Bank Dr.
Palatine   847/963-3032

Schaumburg Township School District 54
524 E. Schaumburg Rd.   847/885-6700

Township High School District 211
1750 S. Roselle Rd.
Palatine   847/755-6600

Community Colleges

Elgin Community College
1700 Spartan Dr.
Elgin   847/888-7377

Harper College
1200 W. Algonquin Rd.
Palatine   847/925-6000

Roosevelt University
Albert A. Robin Campus
1400 N. Roosevelt Blvd.   847/619-8600

Selected Community Organizations

Chicago Atheneum at Schaumburg
190 S. Roselle Rd.   847/895-3950

Children's Advocacy Center
640 Illinois Blvd.   847/885-0100

Department of Health and Human Services
101 Schaumburg Ct. 847/895-4500

Family Counseling Center
217 Civic Dr. 847/524-1505

Northwest Suburban Association of Commerce and Industry (NSACI)
1450 E. American Ln., Ste. 140 847/517-7110

Schaumburg Teen Center
231 Civic Dr. 847/524-3388

Senior Citizens Services
25 Illinois Blvd.
Hoffman Estates 847/884-0030

Spectrum Youth and Family Services
25 Illinois Blvd.
Hoffman Estates 847/884-6212

Twinbrook Family YMCA
300 W. Wise Rd. 847/891-9622

Woodfield Area Charity Organization
1901 N. Roselle Rd., Ste. 800 847/490-5946

Houses of Worship

Bethel Baptist Church
200 N. Roselle Rd. 847/885-3230

Calvary Baptist Church
1000 S. Springinsguth Rd. 847/895-7686

Christ Community Mennonite Church
888 S. Roselle Rd. 847/895-3654

Church of Christ
601 E. Schaumburg Rd. 847/985-0028

Church of the Holy Spirit
1451 Bode Rd.   847/882-7580

Church of Jesus Christ of Latter-Day Saints
1320 W. Schaumburg Rd.   847/882-9889

Church of the Nazarene
1435 W. Wise Rd.   847/529-2345

Covenant Church of Schaumburg
301 N. Meacham Rd.   847/605-8334

First Church of Christ Scientist
603 S. Roselle Rd.   847/895-3695

Holy Land Christian Mission
124 Wilmslow Ln.   847/882-5140

Jehovah's Witnesses
1320 Rodenburg Rd.   630/539-9678

Korean Baptist Church
316 N. Springinsguth Rd.   847/843-0855

Korean Evangelical Church
210 S. Plum Grove Rd.   847/352-0157

Lord of Life Lutheran Church
119 W. Wise Rd.   847/895-8877

Our Redeemer's United Methodist Church
1600 W. Schaumburg Rd.   847/882-6116

Our Savior's United Methodist Church
701 E. Schaumburg Rd.   847/352-8181

Prince of Peace Lutheran Church
930 W. Higgins Rd.   847/885-7010

Salem Korean United Methodist
10 S. Walnut Ln.   847/534-2826

Spring Valley Presbyterian Church
888 S. Roselle Rd.   847/534-0909

DINING

Native's Choices

The Indian Garden
855 E. Schaumburg Rd.
847/524-3007
This little gem is my favorite place for Indian cuisine, from Keralla shrimp to tandoori lobster. Everything is quite authentic, the food is fresh and affordable, and service is great. The kitchen is a marvel, with a large tandoori clay oven where they make their incredible naan bread. Prices range from $7.95 to $16.95.
Open for lunch Mon. - Thurs. 11:30 a.m. - 2:30 p.m., Fri. - Sun. 12 p.m. - 3 p.m.; for dinner Sun. - Thurs. 5 p.m. - 9:45 p.m., Fri. - Sat. 5 p.m. - 10:30 p.m.

Johnny D's
1029 E. Golf Rd.
847/519-9161
After extensive remodeling, Johnny D's is ready to take the area by storm. The pizza is awesome and you can see it baked in the open ovens in back. The front of the house is stylish and happening, and the large selection of Italian and American specialties is boggling. This is an extremely popular spot for good reason and you can even have some unique breakfasts here. Prices range from $7.95 to $18.95.
Open Sun. - Thurs. 7 a.m. - 10 p.m., Fri. - Sat. 7 a.m. - 11 p.m.

Lou Malnati's Pizzeria
1 S. Roselle Rd., 847/985-1525
1050 E. Higgins Rd., Elk Grove Village, 847/439-2000
85 S. Buffalo Grove Rd., Buffalo Grove, 847/215-7100
This is a small, local chain that features great deep-dish pizza and heaping plates of Italian fare in a sports club atmosphere. Prices are average, about $8.95 to $16.95, and service is generally good, although crowds get thick at peak times.
Open Mon. - Sat. 11 a.m. - 11 p.m., Sun. 12 p.m. - 11 p.m.

Vinny's Family Style Italian
Woodfield Mall
847/413-0990
Another of the Carlucci family's creations (see Carlucci in *Rosemont*, p. 108), Vinny's offers an excellent and creative range of Italian entrees ($8.95-$15.95), and pizzas baked in an open hearth are visible to diners. My favorite place to eat when shopping at Woodfield.
Open Mon. - Thurs. 11 a.m. - 8 p.m., Fri. - Sat. 11 a.m. - 9 p.m., Sun. 11 a.m. - 6 p.m.

Yu's Mandarin
200 E. Golf Rd.
847/882-5340
The food at Yu's is authentic and prepared with obvious care. The fried rice, for instance, is pale and not at all greasy, unlike the dark, soy-soaked versions you'll find at inferior joints. Prices are average, from about $7.95 to $12.95; lunch prices are much lower.
Open Sun. - Thurs. 11:30 a.m. - 10 p.m., Fri. - Sat. 11:30 a.m. - 11 p.m.

Worth Noting

Daruma Japanese & Sushi Bar
1823 W. Golf Rd.
847/882-9700
This is the real deal in Japanese dining, right down to floor seating (there are tables, too, of course). The food is good and the atmosphere is almost tranquil. Prices range from $9.95 to $19.95.
Open for lunch Mon. - Sat. 11:30 a.m. - 2 p.m., for dinner 5 p.m. - 10:30 p.m. Closed Mon.

Harry G's Crab House
801 E. Algonquin Rd.
847/397-7750
The seafood here is fresh and prepared to perfection, presentation is impressive, and service is very good. Prices range from $10.95 to the mid-$20s.
Open Mon. - Fri. 11:30 a.m. - 12 a.m., Sat. 4 p.m. - 12 a.m., Sun. 4 p.m. - 10 p.m.

John's Garage
Woodfield Mall
847/619-0046
If you're shopping during one of the busier seasons, you're guaranteed to see a line of people waiting to get into John's Garage. It's not so much that the food is amazing or anything, but it's just about the only place in the mall you'll find great stuffed potato skins and a friendly bar. The line usually moves quickly, so it's worth the wait. Prices range from $5.95 to $16.95.
Open Mon. - Fri. 11 a.m. - 9:30 p.m., Sat. 11 a.m. - 7:30 p.m., Sun. 11 a.m. - 6:30 p.m.

Maggiano's Little Italy
1901 E. Woodfield Rd.
847/240-5600
Maggiano's is part of a small (soon to be big, we suspect) national chain, but we can't help but be impressed by its absolutely gluttonous portions and outstanding service. Two people could honestly get away with ordering one salad and one entree, but why miss the leftovers? An excellent wine list tops off the experience. Prices range from $10.95 to about $24.
Open Mon. - Thurs. 11:15 a.m. - 10 p.m., Fri. 11:15 a.m. - 11 p.m., Sat. 11:45 a.m. - 11 p.m., Sun. 12 p.m. - 9 p.m.

Streamwood's Veterans Memorial

Scenes from Streamwood's Veterans Memorial, one of the few to honor veterans from all wars.

STREAMWOOD

Streamwood at a Glance

Incorporated: 1957
Population: 34,258
Median Household Income: $73,957
Median Home Value: $148,350

Streamwood is one of the more geographically diverse suburbs. Much of the business base of the community, like Elgin, Hoffman Estates, and Schaumburg, is made up of strip malls. But to the immediate west of the village stands a large, beautiful forest preserve that is home to a variety of species of flora and fauna.

About 35,000 people live in Streamwood, where the median household income is between $70,000 and $80,000, and most houses sell for around $150,000—there are a lot of townhomes in the village, which keeps the median price low. Single-family detached homes are closer to $200,000.

One of the central focuses of the village is the Veterans Memorial on Irving Park Road in front of the Village Hall. This moving site is one of the few in the nation which honors all veterans, including women, from all armed conflicts.

Just down the street from the memorial is Hoosier Grove Park, which features a 100-year-old barn, a one-room schoolhouse that now serves as a museum, and a 1950s farmer's garden.

If you've ever wondered where those plastic faux garden pots and containers in your garden are from, it's likely they were made by Duraco Products, headquartered on Lake Street in Streamwood. AWANA Clubs International, a Christian youth organization, also makes its home here.

The vast majority of restaurants in Streamwood are fast-food chains, fast-food independents, or places like Applebee's and Chi-Chi's. Still, a couple of places stand out from the crowd.

ESSENTIAL CONTACTS

Basics

Village of Streamwood
301 E. Irving Park Rd.   630/837-0200

Streamwood Chamber of Commerce
1424 Yorkshire Dr.   630/837-5200

Police Department (non-emergency)
401 E. Irving Park Rd.   630/837-0953

Fire Department (non-emergency)
1095 Schaumburg Rd.   630/213-6300

Police, Fire, and Ambulance (emergency)   911

Townships

Hanover Township
8N180 Rt. 59
Bartlett   630/837-0301

Parks and Recreation

Hoosier Grove Barn and Schoolhouse Museum
700 W. Irving Park Rd.   630/213-3276

Streamwood Park District
777 Bartlett Rd.   630/372-7275

Libraries

Branch library
4300 Audrey Ln.
Hanover Park   630/372-0052

Poplar Creek Library District
1405 S. Park Ave.   630/837-6800

Schools

School Districs

Schaumburg School District 54
524 E. Schaumburg Rd.
Schaumburg   847/885-6700

School District Unit 46
355 E. Chicago St.
Elgin   847/888-5040

Private Elementary Schools

St. John Evangelist Catholic School
513 Parkside Cir.   630/289-3040

Private High Schools

St. Edward High School
335 Locust St.
Elgin   630/741-7535

Community Colleges

Elgin Community College
1700 Spartan Dr.
Elgin   847/888-7385

Selected Community Organizations

Alliance for the Mentally Ill of Hanover
Hanover Township Hall
8N180 Rt. 59
Bartlett   630/837-8875
Support and advocacy for those suffering from mental illness.

Big Brothers/Big Sisters of Fox Valley
158 E. Chicago St.
Elgin   847/888-3111
Mentor program for area youth.

Family Service Association of Greater Elgin
500 S. Bartlett Rd.   630/837-8553

Hospice of Northeastern Illinois
410 S. Hager Ave.
Barrington   847/381-5599
Medicare-certified hospice program serves terminally ill patients and
provides grief support for families of the terminally ill.

Literacy Volunteers of America
200 N. Grove Ave.
Elgin   847/742-6565
Confidential assistance and training for functionally illiterate people of
all ages.

Open Door Clinic of Greater Elgin
164 Division St.
Elgin   847/695-1093
Clinical diagnosis and education related to sexually transmitted
diseases, including HIV.

Streamwood Behavioral Health Center
1400 E. Irving Park Rd.   630/837-9000
Mental health and substance abuse services.

Streamwood Historical Society
777 Bartlett Rd.   630/213-9706

Streamwood Junior Women's Club
P.O. Box 152
Streamwood, IL 60107   630/497-3110
Open to all women over the age of 18.

Houses of Worship

Advent Lutheran Church
1220 E. Irving Park Rd.   630/837-8050

Celebration Community Church
Call for current location of services.   630/830-5948

Faith Missionary Baptist Church
34 W. Streamwood Blvd.   630/697-0731

Grace Bible Church of Streamwood
500 E. Streamwood Blvd.   630/289-1358

Grace Lutheran Church of Streamwood
780 Bartlett Rd.   630/289-3996

Immanuel United Church of Christ
1500 Old Church Rd.   630/837-0190

Poplar Creek Community Church
Call for current location of services.   630/483-1000

St. John's the Evangelist
Park Blvd. and Parkside Cir.   630/837-6500

World Overcomers Church
810 S. Bartlett Rd.
Call for current location of services.   630/830-0933

DINING

Native's Choices

Boulevard Bar & Grill
7 W. Streamwood Blvd.
630/830-2565
The Boulevard is a popular enough place for lunch, but evening is when things really start jumping and where you'll find the most locals. Prices for the above-average bar menu start around $5.95.
Open Sun. - Thurs. 10 a.m. - 1 a.m. (Sun. closing time may vary based on crowd.), Fri. - Sat. 10 a.m. - 2 a.m.

HOFFMAN ESTATES

Hoffman Estates at a Glance

Incorporated: 1959
Population: 48,708
Median Household Income: $70,407
Median Home Value: $180,000

About 50,000 people and 10,000 strip malls fill this oddly-shaped village, roughly bordered by South Barrington to the north, cradled by Schaumburg to the east and south, with Streamwood and Elgin to the west.

The number of strip malls, of course, is an extreme exaggeration. But it would not be an exaggeration to say that most of the village's retail base is found within strip malls along Golf, Algonquin, and Higgins roads. With all the shopping going on, traffic can get thick at times along the main thoroughfares.

Retail stores may be one of the most visual aspects of the village, but some major corporations have made their national headquarters here, including Sears, Roebuck & Co.; Ameritech; and Siemens, a medical imaging systems company.

While a relatively small area, the village boasts more than 50 local parks and almost 4,000 acres of forest preserve land, most of which lies along the western border.

The schools generally rank well above state averages in test scores and graduation rates.

The bulk of restaurants in town are mega-chains or take-out joints, but there are some notable exceptions.

ESSENTIAL CONTACTS

Basics

Village of Hoffman Estates
1900 Hassell Rd.   847/882-9100

Hoffman Estates Chamber of Commerce
2200 W. Higgins Rd., #315   847/781-9100

Police Department (non-emergency)   847/882-1818

Fire Department (non-emergency)   847/882-1818

Police, Fire, and Ambulance (emergency)   911

Townships

Palatine Township
721 S. Quentin Rd.
Palatine   847/358-6700

Schaumburg Township
25 Illinois Blvd.   847/884-0030

Parks and Recreation

Hoffman Estates Park District
1685 W. Higgins Rd.   847/885-7500

Libraries

Hoffman Estates branch
1890 Hassell Rd. (in Village Hall)   847/885-3511

North Hoffman Estates branch
1262 Freeman Rd.   847/934-0220

Schaumburg Township District Library
130 S. Roselle Rd.
Schaumburg   847/985-4000

Schools

School Districts

Community Unit School District 220
310 E. James St.
Barrington   847/381-6300

Elgin School District U46
355 E. Chicago St.
Elgin   847/888-5000

Palatine Community Consolidated School District 15
580 N. First Bank Dr.
Palatine   847/963-3032

Schaumburg Township School District 54
524 E. Schaumburg Rd.
Schaumburg   847/885-6700

Township High School District 211
1750 S. Roselle Rd.
Palatine   847/755-6600

Community Colleges

Harper College
1200 W. Algonquin Rd.
Palatine   847/925-6000

Houses of Worship

Abundant Life Worship Center
1837 Bristol Walk   847/397-4673

Alliance Fellowship Church
665 Grand Canyon St.   847/885-8183

Baha'i Faith
1688 Kingsdale Rd.   847/885-2172

Christian Church of Hoffman Estates
695 Illinois Blvd.   847/885-3683

Christian Temple Of Revelation
1745 Pebblewood Ln.   847/963-8903

Church of the Cross
475 W. Higgins Rd.   847/885-1199

Church of the Holy Innocents
425 Illinois Blvd.   847/885-7900

Destiny Church
325 Illinois Blvd.   847/885-2908

Living Bread Ministries
275 W. Higgins Rd.   847/882-8715

New Life Lutheran Church
1500 W. Algonquin Rd.   847/934-1675

St. Hubert Church
729 Grand Canyon St.   847/885-7700

DINING

Native's Choices

Café Clemenza
1736 W. Algonquin Rd.
847/358-3391
Café Clemenza's great Italian food in a comfortably lively atmosphere
draws a crowd every day. Prices are low—in the $7.95 to $12.95

range, but come hungry.
Open Mon. - Thurs. 11:30 a.m. - 9:45 p.m., Fri. 11:30 a.m. -
10:45 p.m., Sat. 4 p.m. - 10:45 p.m., Sun. 4 p.m. - 8:45 p.m.

Jockey Wok 'n Rolls Restaurant
1017 N. Roselle Rd.
847/885-0888
Ignore the silly name; the food is absolutely superb at this somewhat
upscale Chinese spot tucked behind, you guessed it, a strip mall. The
owner/chef borrowed the name of the restaurant from where he learned
his craft, the famed Jockey Restaurant in Beijing, China.
Open Sun. - Thurs. 11:30 a.m. - 9:30 p.m., Fri. - Sat. 11:30 a.m. -
10:30 p.m.

Magilla's Café
1624 W. Algonquin Rd.
847/963-1621
The phrase "you can't tell a book by its cover" was made for this
little gem tucked away in yet another strip mall. One side of the café
is an outstanding deli and butcher shop; the other side is a bright,
comfortable restaurant reminiscent of a diner. But the food—steaks
and seafood—is strictly top-notch at prices that can't be beat, and
the folks in the small bar in back will make you feel like a regular.
Open Mon. - Sat. 11:30 a.m. - 10 p.m., Sun. 11:30 a.m. - 7 p.m.

Worth Noting

Dover Straits
1149 W. Gannon Dr.
847/884-3900
See sister location in *Mundelein*, p. 194.
Dover Straits has some of the freshest seafood around at prices that
won't make you seasick. A good choice for an afternoon business lunch
or a pleasantly romantic place for two at night. Special prices available
for early evening customers.
Open Mon. - Fri. 11 a.m. - 11 p.m., Sat. 4 p.m. - 12 a.m., Sun. 1 p.m. -
10 p.m.

Official's Time Out Sports Bar
2354 W. Higgins Rd.
847/310-3227
The burgers and appetizers like buffalo wings and skins are the best bet on the simple, but appealing, bar-style menu. More than 20 televisions offer almost any sport you care to watch. A very popular after-work meeting spot.
Open Mon. - Fri. 11 a.m. - 1 a.m., Sat. 11 a.m. - 2 a.m., Sun. 11 a.m. - 12 a.m.

Spring Garden
1000 N. Roselle Rd.
847/882-4912
It's 3 a.m. and you have an inexplicable urge for a large Greek salad and soup. Or maybe it's a burger and fries with a large vanilla milk shake. Either way, this is the place to go if only because there aren't many other places nearby open 24 hours a day. Most prices fall under $10.
Open daily 24 hours.

NORTH BY NORTHWEST

Libertyville, Mundelein, and Vernon Hills

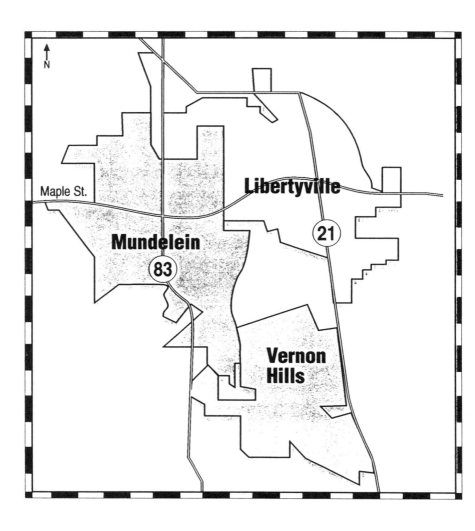

RIVERWOODS

Riverwoods at a Glance

Incorporated: 1959
Population: 3,516
Median Household Income: $262,400
Median Home Value: $510,000

Riverwoods is primarily a bedroom community that shares most of its village services with neighboring Deerfield and Bannockburn. A handful of corporations call Riverwoods home, but the bulk of the village is comprised of large, wooded residential lots with homes valued at $250,000 and up.

ESSENTIAL CONTACTS

Basics

Riverwoods Village Hall
300 Portwine Rd.   847/945-3990

Deerfield, Bannockburn, Riverwoods Chamber of Commerce
747 Deerfield Rd., Ste. LL600   847/945-4660

Police (non-emergency)
Lake County Sheriff (general information)   847/680-3550

Fire Department (non-emergency)
Vernon Fire Protection District   847/634-2512

Police, Fire, and Ambulance (emergency)   911

Townships

Deerfield Township
858 Waukegan Rd.   847/945-0614

Parks and Recreation

Deerfield Park District
836 Jewett Park Dr.
Deerfield   847/945-0650

Libraries

Deerfield Public Library
920 Waukegan Rd.   847/945-3311

Schools

School Districts

Bannockburn Elementary School District 106
2165 Telegraph Rd.   847/945-5900

Deerfield Elementary District 109
517 Deerfield Rd.   847/945-1844

Deerfield High School District 113
1959 Waukegan Rd.   847/432-6510

Stevenson High School District 125
1 Stevenson Dr.
Lincolnshire   847/634-4000

Private Elementary Schools

Holy Cross Catholic - Elementary & Junior High School
720 Elder Ln.   847/945-0135

Community Colleges

College of Lake County
19351 W. Washington St.
Grayslake   847/233-6601

Selected Community Organizations

Arts in Riverwoods   847/914-0109
An invitational exhibit of fine art held in autumn.

Deerfield Area Historical Society
Deerfield and Kipling roads
Deerfield   847/948-0680

Deerfield Golf Course Clubhouse
1201 Sauders Rd.
Riverwoods   847/945-8333

Houses of Worship

Addresses are in Deerfield unless otherwise noted.

Calvary Way Community Church
420 Lake-Cook Rd.   847/948-1180

Christ United Methodist Church of Deerfield
600 Deerfield Rd.   847/945-3040

Community Christian Church Disciples of Christ
1970 Riverwoods Rd.
Lincolnshire   847/945-8824

Congregational Church of Deerfield
225 Wilmot Rd.   847/945-0176

First Church of Christ Scientist
155 Deerfield Rd.   847/945-1626

First Presbyterian Church of Deerfield
824 Waukegan Rd.   847/945-0560

Holy Cross Church
724 Elder Ln.   847/945-0430

Korean Bible Church
1970 Riverwoods Rd.
Lincolnshire   847/948-0208

North Shore Chinese Church
1250 N. Waukegan Rd.   847/945-6760

North Shore Unitarian Church
2100 Half Day Rd.   847/234-2460

North Suburban Evangelical Free Church
200 Lake-Cook Rd.   847/945-4630

St. Gregory's Episcopal Church
Deerfield and Wilmot roads   847/945-1678

Trinity United Church of Christ
760 North St.   847/945-5050

True Way Presbyterian Church
445 Pine St.   847/317-9667

Zen Buddhist Temple of Chicago
865 Bittersweet Dr.
Northbrook   847/272-2070

Zion Evangelical Lutheran Church
10 Deerfield Rd.   847/945-2009

Congregation Beth Judea (Conservative)
Rt. 83 and Hilltop Rd.
Long Grove   847/634-0777

Congregation B'nai Shalom (Traditional)
701 W. Aptakisic Rd.
Buffalo Grove   847/541-1460

Congregation Mishpaha (Reform)
Call for meeting place.   847/459-3279

Congregation Shirat Emet (Reform)
Call for meeting place.   847/541-7273

Lubavitch Chabad (Orthodox)
16296 W. Aptakisic Rd.
Prairie View   847/808-7770

Moriah Congregation
200 Taub Dr.   847/948-5340

Project Seed of Suburban Chicago (Orthodox)
158 McHenry Rd.
Buffalo Grove   847/215-7664

Temple Chai (Reform)
1670 Checker Rd.
Long Grove   847/537-1771

Temple Shir Shalom (Reform)
325 Lexington Dr.
Buffalo Grove   847/465-0101

LINCOLNSHIRE
AND HALF DAY

Lincolnshire at a Glance

Incorporated: 1957
Population: 5,914
Median Household Income: $170,811
Median Home Value: $491,529

The village of Half Day has its roots in the earliest history of the suburbs. It was named for a friendly Potawatomi Indian chief, Halfda. Later, when a government map maker was recording the name, he spelled it "Half Day," apparently under the impression that such was the intention of local residents.

It wasn't until the 1950s that a portion of the property in the area was purchased and developed as a subdivision named Lincolnshire. The area was incorporated as a village in 1957. A small, unincorporated area called Half Day still exists on the fringes of Lincolnshire. Like Hawthorn Woods and Kildeer, Lincolnshire is mostly a bedroom community with little retail base but substantial economic support from industrial and corporate firms, as well as the sprawling Marriott's Lincolnshire Resort.

The resort itself is sort of a central focus for the community; its high-quality professional theater and golf courses serve as many residents as visitors, as do its four restaurants and large banquet spaces.

Most of the village's 5,600 residents are professionals employed at nearby corporations such as the Quill Corporation, Hewitt Associates, Abbott Laboratories, and various business parks; the median household income is around $170,000.

Nightlife is scarce in the village, although the recent opening of the

Lincolnshire movie theater, with 20 screens and an IMAX theater, has at least created something to do after hours. The large, nautically-themed cocktail lounge at the resort is also quite crowded on weekends and often features live music.

There are a handful of restaurants in the immediate area of the resort, the oldest being the Half Day Inn. This, and Flatlander's, are the places you'll find most of the action on weekends.

ESSENTIAL CONTACTS

Basics

Village Hall
1 Olde Half Day Rd.   847/883-8600

South Central Lake County Chamber of Commerce
175 Olde Half Day Rd.   847/993-2409

Police Department
1 Olde Half Day Rd.   847/883-9900

Fire Department
Lincolnshire-Riverwoods Fire Protection District
115 Schelter Rd.   847/634-2512

Townships

Vernon Township
3050 N. Main St.
Prairie View   847/634-4600

Parks and Recreation

Park District
1 Olde Half Day Rd.   847/883-8600

Schools

School Districts

Elementary School District 103
1370 Riverwoods Rd.
Lake Forest   847/295-4030

High School District 125
1 Stevenson Dr.   847/634-4000

Selected Community Organizations

Friends of Ryerson Woods
Ryerson Conservation Area
21950 N. Riverwoods Rd.
Deerfield   847/948-7750

League of Women Voters (Deerfield/Lincolnshire)
P.O. Box 124
Deerfield, IL 60015   847/945-2964

Lincolnshire Community Association
P.O. Box 705
Lincolnshire, IL 60069   847/945-3811

Lincolnshire Garden Club   847/405-0703

Riverside Foundation Auxiliary   847/945-9675

Village Club of Lincolnshire (Newcomers club) 847/945-2872

Houses of Worship

Community Christian Church
1970 Riverwoods Rd.   847/945-8824

Korean Bible Church
1970 Riverwoods Rd.   847/948-0208

Lutheran Church of the Holy Spirit
30 Riverwoods Rd.   847/945-1550

Village Church Of Lincolnshire
201 Riverwoods Rd.   847/295-7707

Washburn Congregational Church
240 Olde Half Day Rd.   847/821-8625

DINING

Native's Choices

Marriott's Lincolnshire Theater
847/634-0200 (performance and ticket information)
The professional theater at Marriott's Lincolnshire Resort is one of
the finest venues in the suburbs. The "in-the-round" setting may be
a challenge for actors, but the sound and sight-lines make it a treat
for audiences. Most often, musicals are the choice, and it's rare for
the troupes here to hit a bad note.

Flatlander's Restaurant and Brewery
200 Village Green
847/821-1234
The combination of excellent house brews, good food, and live music
after 9 p.m. Thursday through Saturday make this hot spot tough to
beat. The food covers a wide range of American styles, from burgers to
top-quality steaks, poultry, and seafood. Prices from $7.95 to $18.95.
*Open for lunch Mon. - Fri. 11:30 a.m. - 2:30 p.m., Sat. 12 p.m. -
2:30 p.m., Sun. brunch 10 a.m. - 2 p.m.; for dinner Mon. - Thurs.
4:30 p.m. - 10:30 p.m., Fri. 4:30 p.m. - 11 p.m., Sat. 3:30 p.m. -
11 p.m., Sun. 3:30 p.m. - 10 p.m.*

Tacos Del Rey
23250 N. Milwaukee Ave.
Half Day
847/634-1530
Tacos Del Rey is one of those unexpectedly pleasant surprises that
crop up from time to time on the restaurant beat. The standard list of

Mexican fare is prepared quickly and well; you can bet locals eat here all the time. Prices are low; just about everything is under $10.
Open Mon. - Sat. 9 a.m. - 9 p.m., Sun. 11 a.m. - 6 p.m.

Half Day Inn
Milwaukee Ave. (Rt. 21) and Rt. 45
Half Day
847/634-8118
The pub-style grub and large, welcoming bar makes this one of the more popular eateries north of Lake-Cook Road. Prices, beginning at $5.95, are low, too. Pizza and burgers are the most popular items on the menu.
Kitchen open daily 11 a.m. - 9:30 p.m., bar open Mon. - Thurs. 11 a.m. - 3 a.m., Fri. - Sat. 11 a.m. - 4 a.m.

VERNON HILLS

Vernon Hills at a Glance

Incorporated: 1958
Population: 17,792
Median Income: $70,854
Median Home Value: $189,925

If you stick to the main roads of Vernon Hills, you might be tempted to wonder where the 18,000 residents actually live. The main roads are filled mostly with strip malls, Hawthorne Center shopping mall, and office buildings—most people live on the village's south and west sides.

While there is no true "town center" in the village, local officials are carefully planning future land uses with an eye toward the creation of healthy communities. The large amount of retail in Vernon Hills keeps taxes low, and housing prices are among the most reasonable in east Lake County. That fact, combined with the convenient access to major highways and rail lines, make it a popular place to live.

ESSENTIAL CONTACTS

Basics

Vernon Hills Village Hall
290 Evergreen Dr.   847/367-3700

LMV Chamber of Commerce
731 N. Milwaukee Ave.
Libertyville   847/680-0750

Police Department (non-emergency)
754 Lakeview Pkwy.   847/362-4449

Countryside Fire Protection District (non-emergency)
600 N. Deerpath Dr.   847/367-5511

Lincolnshire-Riverwoods Fire Protection District (non-emergency)
115 Schelter Rd.
Lincolnshire   847/634-2512

Police, Fire, and Ambulance (emergency)   911

Townships

Vernon Township
3050 N. Main St.
Prairie View   847/634-4600

Parks and Recreation

Vernon Hills Park District
Delores C. Sullivan Center
635 Aspen Dr.   847/367-7270

Libraries

Cook Memorial Library District
413 N. Milwaukee Ave.
Libertyville   847/362-2330

Vernon Area Library District
300 Olde Half Day Rd.
Lincolnshire   847/634-3650

Schools

School Districts

Diamond Lake School District 76
25807 Diamond Lake Rd.
Mundelein   847/566-9221

Hawthorn District 73 Schools (K-8)
201 Hawthorn Pkwy.   847/367-3226

Kildeer Countryside District 96
1050 Ivy Hall Ln.
Buffalo Grove   847/459-4260

Libertyville High School District 128
708 W. Park Ave.
Libertyville   847/367-3110

Stevenson High School District 125
1 Stevenson Dr.
Lincolnshire   847/634-4000

Private High Schools

Carmel High School
One Carmel Pkwy.
Mundelein   847/566-3000

SITES

Cuneo Museum and Gardens
1350 N. Milwaukee Ave.
847/362-3042
This unique property has the distinction of having been featured in the
film *My Best Friend's Wedding*, starring Julia Roberts. You won't find
any celebrities here now, but you can see a wonderful art collection and
formal gardens surrounding a turn-of-the-century mansion. The Cuneo
site is also home to occasional stage productions, with daily tours and
Sunday brunches available. Also a popular wedding site during spring
and summer months.

DINING

Native's Choices

Cafe Pyrenees
701 N. Milwaukee Ave.
847/918-8850
In terms of elegance, preparation, and cuisine, the French country style of Cafe Pyrenees is unbeatable. Truly a top-notch restaurant, dress is business casual. Prices range from the mid-teens and up.
Open for lunch Tues. - Fri. 11:30 a.m. - 2 p.m.; for dinner Tues. - Fri. 5:30 p.m. - 9 p.m., Sat. 5 p.m. - 10 p.m. Closed Sun. - Mon.

Tsukasa, Japanese Steak and Seafood
700 N. Milwaukee Ave.
847/816-8770
Tsukasa is arguably the best of all the Japanese steakhouses in the suburbs. All of the usual ingredients are here: a master blade-thrower behind the tableside grill, fresh ingredients, and a good bar, but somehow it all comes together just a little bit nicer than others of the kind. Prices range from $11.95 to $16.95.
Open for lunch Tues. - Fri. 11:30 a.m. - 2 p.m.; for dinner Tues. - Thurs. 5 p.m. - 9:30 p.m., Fri. 5 p.m. - 10:30 p.m., Sat. 5 p.m. - 10:30 p.m., Sun. 4 p.m. - 9 p.m.

Worth Noting

Angelo's
906 S. Rt. 45
847/918-9442
Angelo's is a popular steak and seafood place. The menu is filled with mostly American standards, but the preparation and service keep people coming back. Prices range from $10.95 to $21.95.
Open Mon. - Sat. 11 a.m. - 11 p.m., Sun. 4 p.m. - 10 p.m.

On The Border
535 Lakeview Pkwy.
847/918-8235
On The Border is, hands down, the most popular and best Tex-Mex grill in the area. The fajitas and chili put those chain places to shame. Prices range from $8.95 to $14.95.
Restaurant open Sun. - Thurs. 11 a.m. - 10 p.m., Fri. - Sat. 11 a.m. - 12 a.m.; bar open nightly one hour later than the kitchen.

Pizzeria Uno
545 Lakeview Pkwy.
847/918-8667
OK, OK, so it's a chain that properly belongs in Chicago, but who cares? This is still *the* place to go when you're in the mood for a deep-dish pizza and to avoid the huge crowd that fills the downtown version. Better be hungry. Prices for pizzas start in the mid-teens. Why even bother with anything else?
Open Mon. - Thurs. 11 a.m. - 11 p.m., Fri. - Sat. 11 a.m. - 1 a.m., Sun. 11 a.m. - 10 p.m.

Silk Mandarin
4 E. Phillip Rd.
847/680-1760
The parking lot is usually full at this unpretentious little Chinese restaurant featuring basic selections of Hunan, Canton, and Szechuan. Service is fast, and ingredients are always fresh. Prices range from $5.95 to $12.95.
Open Mon. - Thurs. 11:30 a.m. - 10 p.m., Fri. - Sat. 11:30 a.m. - 11 p.m., Sun. 11:30 a.m. - 9 p.m.

Sushi Masa
701 N. Milwaukee Ave.
847/549-0101
One of the precious few authentic sushi bars north of Lake-Cook Road also serves very good cooked Japanese food. I've always enjoyed my experience here, and it's fun to watch the sushi chef do his thing. Prices start around $7.95; lunches are a couple of dollars less.
Open for lunch Mon. - Fri. 11:30 a.m. - 4 p.m.; for dinner Mon. - Fri. 5 p.m. - 9:30 p.m., Sat. 4 p.m. - 10 p.m. Closed Sun.

The campus of the University of St. Mary's of the Lake in Mundelein.

MUNDELEIN

Mundelein at a Glance

Incorporated: 1924
Population: 28,012
Median Household Income: $68,401
Median Home Value: $166,000

When in 1835 Peter Shaddle first built his cabin on the property that now holds St. Mary of the Lake Seminary, the lands nearby were comprised of vast prairies and marshes. The first recorded name of the settlement is "Mechanic's Grove," named by English immigrants who built much of the original community.

Like neighboring Libertyville, the town went through a number of name changes. From "Holcomb," after one of the area's first developers, it changed to "Rockefeller," after the 20th century railroad magnate, and then to "Area," named by an acronymically-conscious entrepreneur for his sales philosophy: Ability, Reliability, Endurance, and Action.

In 1924, village leaders decided to honor George Cardinal Mundelein, who had purchased and developed St. Mary of the Lake Seminary. Many of the downtown buildings from this time are still standing, including the Village Hall, which was built in 1929.

Over the past 20 years, the growth of Mundelein and the surrounding villages has been impressive. Northeastern Illinois Planning Commission statistics suggest that as many as 35,000 residents will inhabit Mundelein by 2010, up from about 21,000 in 1990.

The village seems to have struck a careful balance between the image of a quaint bedroom community and a thriving business center. A drive up busy Milwaukee Avenue offers a look at Mundelein's commercial heart, but a quick trip down almost any side street reveals long, quiet blocks filled with mature trees and homes, most of which sell for around $165,000.

ESSENTIAL CONTACTS

Basics

Mundelein Village Hall
440 E. Hawley St.   847/949-3200

LMV Area Chamber of Commerce
731 N. Milwaukee Ave.
Libertyville   847/680-0750

Mundelein MainStreet
16 E. Park Ave.   847/970-9235
A downtown revitalization program for Mundelein

Police Department (non-emergency)
200 N. Seymour Ave.   847/949-3250

Fire Department (non-emergency)
169 N. Seymour Ave.   847/949-3260

Police, Fire, and Ambulance (emergency)   911

Parks and Recreation

Lake County Forest Preserves
2000 N. Milwaukee Ave.
Libertyville   847/367-6640

Mundelein Park District
601 Noel Dr.   847/566-8122

Libraries

Cook Memorial Library District
413 N. Milwaukee Ave.
Libertyville   847/362-2330

Fremont Public Library District
470 N. Lake St.   847/566-8702

Friends of the Fremont Library
450 N. Lake Shore Dr.   847/566-6281

Schools

School Districts

Diamond Lake School District 76
500 Acorn Ln.
Diamond Lake   847/566-9221

Fremont School District 79
28855 N. Fremont Center Rd.   847/566-0169

Hawthorn School District
201 Hawthorn Pkwy.
Vernon Hills   847/367-3244

Libertyville High School District 128
708 W. Park Ave.   847/367-3110

Mundelein Elementary School District 75
200 W. Maple Ave.   847/949-2700

Mundelein High School District 120
1350 W. Hawley St.   847/949-2200

Private Elementary Schools

Santa Maria del Popolo School
126 N. Lake St.   847/949-2335

Private High Schools

Carmel High School
1 Carmel Pkwy.   847/566-3000

Selected Community Organizations

American Association of Retired Persons (AARP), Chapter 2255
793 Beach Pl.   847/566-1767

Audubon Society of Lake County
206 W. Maple
Libertyville   847/362-7053

Bicycle Club of Lake County
P.O. Box 521
Libertyville, IL 60048   847/604-0520

Boy Scouts of America
2745 Skokie Valley Rd.
Highland Park   847/433-1813

Breakfast Exchange of LMV   847/949-1981
A service organization working towards the prevention of child abuse.

Business and Professional Women's Club
618 N. Norton Ave.   847/566-7409

Camera Club of Lake County
419 Northgate Rd.
Lindenhurst   847/566-1373

Historical Society of Fort Hill Country
P.O. Box 249
Wauconda   847/526-7556

Historical Society (Libertyville/Mundelein)
502 E. Rockland Rd.
Libertyville   847/362-4654

Home and Garden Club of Libertyville/Mundelein
433 Flanders Ln.
Grayslake   847/223-9648

Mundelein Elves (4H Club)
851 Glenview Ave.   847/949-0089

Mundelein/Libertyville Chess Club
507 Greenview Ave.   847/566-6938

Kirk Players (theater group)
224 Forest Ln.   847/566-6594

Moraine Girl Scout Council
155 Pfingsten Rd., Ste. 201
Deerfield   847/945-7750

Mundelein Community Women's Club
364 Banbury Rd.   847/566-1347

Mundelein Senior Center
1200 Regent Dr.   847/566-4790

Mundelein Women's League
1014 Evergreen St.   847/949-6454

Welcome Wagon   800/359-9056,
                                            x. 7033

SITES

Fort Hill Heritage Museum
601 Noel Dr.
Mundelein
847/526-7566
Monthly meeting held on the fourth Thursday of each month at the
Mundelein Senior Center (1200 Regent Dr.).
Open Sat. 1 p.m. - 4 p.m., except Jan. - Feb.

St. Mary of the Lake Seminary
1000 E. Maple Ave.
847/566-6401 (seminary)
847/566-8290 (Center for Development in Ministry)
While not touted as a tourist destination for obvious reasons, St. Mary
of the Lake Seminary remains one of the most scenic locales in the
entire Chicago metropolitan region. The 14 buildings that make up the
campus overlook a serene lake; the sense of peace and stillness here is

overwhelming.

The original university was established in the city of Chicago in 1844 by the city's first bishop, William Quarter.

George Cardinal Mundelein acquired the Mundelein property in 1921, built the school at a cost of $10 million, and relocated the Catholic theological university shortly thereafter. The school has facilities for about 400 students; less than 200 are currently enrolled.

The extensive Feehan Memorial Library is both beautiful and impressive with more than 150,000 theological and philosophical books, several dating from the 16th and 17th centuries, and a number of periodicals not otherwise readily available. The interior of the building is architecturally dramatic, with a large marble staircase at the entrance and intricate wood craftsmanship throughout.

The library is open to the public, but visitors must check in at the office.
Open Mon. - Fri. 8 a.m. - 4:30 p.m.

DINING

Native's Choices

Dover Straits
890 E. U.S. Highway 45,
847/949-1500
See sister location in *Hoffman Estates*, p. 167.
Dover Straits has some of the freshest seafood around at prices that won't make you seasick. Keep in mind this area is landlocked when it comes to saltwater choices. The atmosphere is perfect for an afternoon business lunch, especially if your guest likes fish trophies, but it also works at night as a pleasantly romantic place for two. Special prices available for early evening customers.
Open Mon. - Fri. 11 a.m. - 11 p.m., Sat. 4 p.m. - 12 a.m., Sun. 1 p.m. - 10 p.m.

Gilmer Road House
25792 Midlothian Rd.

847/438-0300

Although easy enough to find, the Gilmer Road House is definitely off the beaten track. The pub-like décor is cozy, the customers and staff are friendly, and the food is good, fast, and inexpensive. Most things fall under $10.

Open Mon. - Sat. 11 a.m. - 12 a.m., Sun. 8 p.m. - 10 p.m.

Worth Noting

El Barrio Restaurant and Lounge
1122 Diamond Lake Rd.

847/566-0475

The selections are familiar enough (tacos, burritos, and enchiladas), but the kitchen does a slightly above-average job of preparing and presenting them. Prices are reasonable ($7.95-$12.95), and of Mundelein's many Mexican restaurants, this is the best. The staff is friendly and the interior is strictly casual.

Open for lunch Mon. - Thurs. 11:30 a.m. - 2 p.m.; for dinner Mon. - Thurs. 4:30 p.m. - 9:45 p.m., Sun. 3 p.m. - 9:45 p.m. Open Fri. - Sat. 11:30 a.m. - 10:45 p.m.

Gale Street Inn-Diamond Lake
902 Diamond Lake Rd.

847/566-1090

No longer related to the restaurant of the same name on Chicago's northwest side, this Gale Street still offers much the same fare. That is to say, good ribs and top-rate family fare at reasonable prices. The views of Diamond Lake are outstanding.

Open for lunch Mon. - Sat. 11 a.m. - 3 p.m., for dinner Mon. - Sat. 3 p.m. - 10 p.m., Sun. 12 p.m. - 10 p.m.

LIBERTYVILLE

Libertyville at a Glance

Incorporated: 1841
Population: 19,772
Median Household Income: $95,800
Median Home Value: $266,800

The village of Libertyville retains much of the charm and history of the earliest days of the suburbs.

The town went through several name changes in the early 1800s, from Vardin's Grove to Independence Grove to Burlington when, in 1839, it became the village government seat for Lake County. It wasn't long, however (1841), when the county government moved to Waukegan, and residents decided they liked Libertyville better.

Libertyville and neighboring Mundelein share the benefits of a central county location. That, and assertive efforts to preserve the historic elements of the village has made Libertyville one of the more appealing places to live in Lake County.

The median price for homes is almost $270,000 (though some can still be found in the low $100s), and the excellent school system combined with easy access to nearby corporations makes the village attractive to professionals with children. Still, affordable housing prices and lots of rental properties help keep the median age of the population in the 22 to 35 range.

The arts community is quite active with the David Adler Cultural Center the focal point. The center, formerly the home of a famed Chicago architect, plays host to several arts festivals, folk concerts, and workshops, and a gift shop on the premises offers some wonderful handmade items from jewelry to paper.

If looking at the wonderful old buildings along the village's central corridor Milwaukee Avenue doesn't sate your cravings for history, head to the Ansel B. Cook Victorian Home Museum. Built in 1876, it's really the princess of historic homes in Lake County, and the furniture is all authentic. Generally, it's only open on Sundays during the summer or by appointment.

ESSENTIAL CONTACTS

Basics

Libertyville Village Hall
118 W. Cook Ave.   847/362-2430

LMV Chamber of Commerce
731 N. Milwaukee Ave.   847/680-0750

Police Department (non-emergency)
Schertz Municipal Building
200 E. Cook Ave.   847/362-8310

Fire Department Headquarters (non-emergency)
North Station
1551 N. Milwaukee Ave.   847/362-5664

Townships

Libertyville Township
359 Merrill Ct.   847/816-6800

Parks and Recreation

Libertyville Park District
625 W. Winchester Rd.   847/918-7275

Libraries

Cook Memorial Library District
413 N. Milwaukee Ave.   847/362-2330
Note: Two new library buildings may be built, depending on the
outcome of a 1999 referendum.

Schools

School Districts

Libertyville School District 70
1441 W. Lake St.   847/362-8393

Libertyville School District 128
708 West Park Ave.   847/367-3159

Selected Cultural Organizations

Ansel B. Cook Victorian Home Museum
413 N. Milwaukee Ave.   847/362-2330

David Adler Cultural Center
1600 N. Milwaukee Ave.   847/367-0707

Libertyville Civic Center
135 W. Cook Ave.   847/918-8880

Houses of Worship

Calvary Way Community Church
1117 S. Milwaukee Ave.   847/948-1180

Church Of The Redeemer
Bradley and Old School roads   847/367-7607

Evangelical Free Church
431 W. Austin Ave.   847/362-8155

First Church-Christian Scientist
240 Park Pl.   847/362-5540

First Presbyterian Church
219 W. Maple Ave.   847/362-2174

Grace Lutheran Church
501 Valley Park Dr.   847/367-7050

Hawthorn Hills Community Church
28100 N. Ashley Cir.   847/918-8822

Holy Cross Lutheran Church
29700 N. Saint Mary's Rd.   847/367-4060

Jehovah's Witnesses
575 N. Butterfield Rd.   847/367-8529

Korean Full Gospel Church
1375 Atkinson Rd.   847/918-1700

Libertyville Covenant Church
250 S. Saint Mary's Rd.   847/362-3308

North Shore Christian Church
28085 N. Ashley Cir.   847/362-1085

Reorganized Church of Jesus
835 W. Winchester Rd.   847/362-6956

St John's Lutheran Church
501 W. Park Ave.   847/362-4424

St Joseph's Parish
121 E. Maple Ave.   847/362-2073

St Lawrence's Episcopal Church
125 W. Church St.   847/362-2110

United Methodist Church
429 Brainerd Ave.   847/362-2112

Word Of Faith Community Church
1400 N. Butterfield Rd.   847/816-9331

DINING

Native's Choices

Mickey Finn's
412 N. Milwaukee Ave.
847/362-6688
Mickey Finn's has a strangely wonderful personality, with microbrews,
a lively crowd and staff, and a menu that ranges from great burgers
to Mexican delights. Anywhere else and the menu might be called
schizophrenic. Prices are dirt cheap ($5-$11), though you'll likely
spend a fin or two on the great brews.
*Open Mon. - Thurs. 11 a.m. - 12 a.m. (full menu until 10 p.m., pizzas
until 11 p.m.); Fri. - Sat. 11 a.m. - 1 a.m. (full menu until 11 p.m.,
pizzas until 12 a.m.); Sun. 12 p.m. - 9 p.m.*

Lou Malnati's Pizzeria
1436 S. Milwaukee Ave.
847/362-6070
See listing in *Buffalo Grove*, p. 57.
*Open Mon. - Thurs. 4 p.m. - 10 p.m., Fri. - Sat. 11 a.m. - 11 p.m.,
Sun. 11 a.m. - 9 p.m.*

Worth Noting

Yan's Hunan Inn
911 Lakehurst Rd.
847/473-1660
Probably the best Chinese food north of Rt. 22, Yan's features the
typically wide range of authentic Hunan dishes with fresh ingredients
and lightning service. The flaming combo platter of appetizers is a
popular bet. Prices range from about $7.95 to $15.95.
Open daily 11 a.m. - 9 p.m.

Country Inn of Lambs Farm
I-94 and Rt. 176
847/362-5050
The basic American home-style food is unpretentious, hearty, and good. It's also easy on the pocketbook. Prices range from about $6.95 to $10.95.
Open daily 11 a.m. - 8 p.m.

THE FUN STUFF

CULTURAL OUTINGS

History Lessons
(Museums and Historical Societies)

Exhibitionists (Art Galleries)

The Wheeling Historical Museum in Wheeling.

The original McDonald's restaurant in Des Plaines.

HISTORY LESSONS

Museums and Historical Societies

Arlington Heights Historical Museum
110 W. Fremont St.
Arlington Heights
847/255-1225
847/255-1450 (Musuem Country Store)

Barrington Area Historical Society
218 W. Main St.
Barrington
847/381-1730

Chester Gould/Dick Tracy Museum
Old Courthouse on the Square
101 N. Johnson St.
Woodstock
815/338-8281

Clayson House Museum
224 E. Palatine Rd.
Palatine
847/991-6460

Cuneo Museum and Gardens
1350 N. Milwaukee Ave.
Vernon Hills
847/362-3042

Des Plaines Historical Museum
789 Pearson St.
Des Plaines
847/391-5399

Dietrich Friedrichs Farmhouse Museum
101 S. Maple St.
Mount Prospect
847/392-9006

Elgin Historical Society Museum
350 Park St.
Elgin
847/741-5660

Elgin Public Museum of Natural History
Lords Park
225 Grand Blvd.
Elgin
847/741-6655

Farmhouse Museum
399 Biesterfield Rd.
Elk Grove Village
847/439-3994

JFK Health World
1301 S. Grove Ave.
Barrington
847/842-9100
Children's health education center.

Lake County Museum
Lakewood Forest Preserve
Rt. 176, one block west of Fairfield Rd.
Wauconda
847/526-7878

McHenry County Historical Society Museum
6422 Main St.
Union
815/923-2267

Raupp Memorial Museum
901 Dunham Ln.
Buffalo Grove
847/459-5700, x. 116

Wauconda Historical Society
711 N. Main St.
Wauconda
847/526-9303

Wheeling Historical Museum
251 N. Wolf Road
Wheeling
847/537-0327

EXHIBITIONISTS

ART GALLERIES

Arlington Heights

Dunton Gallery
18 S. Evergreen Ave.
847/818-0694
High-quality, original art of various media with Western and Southwest influences.

Tribal Expressions
7 S. Dunton Ave.
847/590-5390
Original, high-quality Native American art in all media.

Barrington

Accent Art
135 Park Ave.
847/426-8842

Aubrey's of Barrington
Ice House Mall
200 Applebee St.
847/382-3838

Barrington Area Arts Council Gallery
207 Park Ave.
847/382-5626
Exhibits vary monthly.

Barrington Area Arts Council Gallery
Barrington Area Library
505 N. Northwest Hwy.
847/382-5626
Exhibits vary monthly.

Chesterfield Glass Galleries
Ice House Mall
200 Applebee St.
847/382-6677

Clair E. Smith Art Gallery
Barrington High School
616 W. Main St.
847/842-3214
High-quality student art works. Exhibits vary.

Childhede Gallery Ltd.
Westgate Center
442 W. Northwest Hwy.
847/304-1963

Fancy Art N.F.P.
113 E. Main St.
847/304-4045
Primarily fine paintings and prints featuring a number of local artists.

G. Whiz
The Foundry
724 W. Northwest Hwy.
847/304-0255

Graphic Source Art Gallery
Ice House Mall
200 Applebee St.
847/381-2476

Stay Tooned Gallery
Ice House Mall
200 Applebee St.
847/382-2357
Original animated cartoon frames and memorabilia.

Des Plaines

Koehnline Visual Arts Center
Oakton Community College
1600 E. Golf Rd.
847/635-1600

The Studio Gallery
1547 Ellinwood Ave.
847/359-7490

Elgin

E. Max von Isser Gallery
Student Resource Center
Elgin Community College
1700 Spartan Dr.
Elgin
847/697-1000, x. 7405

Gallery of Photographic Art
Visual and Performing Arts Center
Elgin Community College
1700 Spartan Dr.
Elgin
847/697-1000, x. 7405

Safety-Kleen Gallery One
Visual and Performing Arts Center
Elgin Community College
1700 Spartan Drive
Elgin
847/697-1000, x. 7405

Elk Grove Village

Finartin' Collections
1080 Nerge Rd., Ste. 105
847/352-1770

Grayslake

College of Lake County
Community Gallery of Art
19351 W. Washington Blvd.
Grayslake
847/543-2405

Hoffman Estates

Ankh Gallery
1568 W. Algonquin Rd.
847/776-1207

Lake Zurich

Cooley's Custom Framing and Gallery
56 E. Main St.
847/438-8893

Ela Area Public Library
135 S. Buesching Rd.
847/438-3433

Frog Art Gallery
Rand and Quentin roads
847/438-3644
American, European, and Oriental prints from the 19th and 20th
centuries.

Mainstreet Art Center
16 E. Main St.
847/550-0016

Libertyville

David Adler Cultural Center
1700 N. Milwaukee Ave.
847/367-0707
Exhibits featuring local artists vary monthly.

Lincolnshire

Vernon Area Public Library
300 Old Half Day Rd.
847/634-3650

Long Grove

Acclaim Gallery
445 Robert Parker Coffin Rd.
847/478-9192

Artists' Cove
410 Robert Parker Coffin Rd.
847/478-0688

Get Wild, Go Wild
Wildlife and Wilderness Images
309 Old McHenry Rd.
847/478-9383

The Studio of Long Grove
360 Historical Ln.
847/634-4244

Mount Prospect

Tomali Gallery
8 W. Busse Ave.
847/398-1360

Wild Sisters
8A W. Busse Ave.
847/368-0696

Palatine

Frame Corner Fine Art Gallery
34 W. Palatine Rd.
847/991-9281

Rolling Meadows

Art by Carl
2312 Wing St.
847/392-0740

Fitch Galleries
Meadows Town Mall
1400 E. Golf Rd., #120
847/952-8885

Schaumburg

Chicago Athenaeum at Schaumburg
190 S. Roselle Rd.
847/895-3950

Prairie Center for the Arts
201 Schaumburg Ct.
847/895-3600

Wheeling

Delta Stained Glass
75 S. Milwaukee Ave.
847/541-4527

Provenance Gallery and Gifts
971 N. Milwaukee Ave.
847/215-9885
Original art including etchings and hand-colored engravings.

THAT'S ENTERTAINMENT

Popcorn Palaces (Movie Theaters)

Stage Presence (Theaters)

Night on the Town
(Nightclubs, Taverns, and Coffeehouses)

Solo Expeditions (Singles Groups)

The Des Plaines Theater in downtown Des Plaines.

Barrington's Catlow Theater.

POPCORN PALACES

Arlington Heights

Ridge Cinemas
900 W. Dundee Rd.
847/444-FILM, #534

Town & Country Theaters
Palatine and Rand roads
847/444-FILM, #535

Barrington

AMC South Barrington 30
175 Studio Dr.
(I-90 at Barrington Rd.)
847/765-7262

The Catlow Theater
116 W. Main St.
847/381-0777

Des Plaines

Des Plaines Theater
1476 Miner St.
847/298-6715

Elk Grove Village

Elk Grove Theater
Biesterfield and Arlington Heights roads
847/228-6707

Fox Lake

Fox Lake Theater
115 Lakeland Plaza
847/973-2800

Hanover Park

Tradewinds Theater
Barrington and Irving Park roads
630/289-6707

Hoffman Estates

Barrington Square 6
2230 W. Higgins Rd.
847/843-7606

Lake Zurich

The Lake Zurich 12
Rt. 12 east of Ela Rd.
847/550-0000

Libertyville

Libertyville Theater
708 N. Milwaukee Ave.
847/362-3011

Lincolnshire

Citypark 20 & IMAX
300 Parkway Dr.
847/215-2690

Mount Prospect

Randhurst Theater
101 E. Euclid Ave. (adjacent to Randhurst Shopping Center)
847/590-9788

Rolling Meadows

Sony Theater
1701 Algonquin Rd. (at Golf Rd.)
847/952-8200

Schaumburg

Woodfield Theaters
Rt. 53 and I-90
847/444-FILM, #627
847/444-FILM, #597 (Inside the mall)

Streamwood

Sony Theater
1500 Buttitta Dr.
630/289-6900

Vernon Hills

Hawthorne
Routes 60 and 21 (adjacent to Hawthorne Center)
847/444-FILM, #529

River Tree Court
701 N. Milwaukee Ave.
847/444-FILM, #528

Showplace 8
555 N. Lakeview Pkwy.
847/247-8958

The Bog Theatre in Des Plaines.

STAGE PRESENCE

Bartlett

Bartlett Community Theatre
Apple Orchard Community Center
696 W. Stearns Rd.
630/837-6568

Des Plaines

The Bog Theatre
620 Lee St.
847/296-0622

Des Plaines Theatre Guild
Prairie Lakes Community Center
Dempster and Thacker streets
847/391-5720

Elgin

Elgin Community Theater
Theatre 355
355 E. Chicago St.
847/741-0532

Independent Players
Elgin Community College
1700 Spartan Dr.
847/931-5125

Elk Grove

Elk Grove Center for the Performing Arts
847/301-1206
Shows staged in various area venues.

Lincolnshire

Marriott Theatre (professional equity)
Marriott's Lincolnshire Resort
10 Marriott Dr.
847/634-0200

Lisle

Tempo Players
Sacred Heart Monastery
Rt. 53 and Maple Ave.
630/495-8582

Mount Prospect

D.R.A.M.M.A.
The Mount Prospect Theatre Society
RecPlex
420 W. Dempster St.
847/640-1000

Palatine

Harper College Theatre
William Rainey Harper Community College
1200 W. Algonquin Rd.
847/925-6000, x. 6547

Music On Stage
Cutting Hall
150 E. Wood St.
847/991-5990

Village Theatre
Cutting Hall
150 E. Wood St.
847/358-2506

St. Charles

Pheasant Run Theatre
4051 E. Main St.
630/584-6300

Schaumburg

Schaumburg Encore Theatre
Schaumburg Prairie Center for the Arts
201 Schaumburg Ct.
847/895-3600

Wheeling Park Productions
Wheeling Community Recreation Center
333 W. Dundee Rd.
847/465-3333

Vernon Hills

Cuneo Museum and Gardens
1350 N. Milwaukee Ave.
847/362-3042

Woodstock

Town Square Players
The Woodstock Opera House
121 Van Buren St.
815/338-5300

Woodstock Musical Theatre Company
Woodstock Opera House
121 Van Buren St.
815/338-5300

Ye Olde Town Inn in Mount Prospect is one of the friendliest
of the area's neighborhood pubs.

NIGHT ON THE TOWN

Arlington Heights

Bill's Inn
20 E. Northwest Hwy.
847/255-5835
It's dark and often smoky, but Bill's is one of my favorite dive bars
anywhere. Maybe because they serve Guinness Stout at the right
temperature, or maybe because of the erudite bartender, Wally.
Don't even think about food.
Open Mon. - Thurs. 8 a.m. - 12 a.m., Fri. - Sat. 8 a.m. - 1 a.m.

Harry's of Arlington
1 N. Vail Ave.
847/577-2525
One of the top contenders for best suburban "neighborhood pub"
features a better-than-average bar menu, friendly crowds, occasional
live music on weekends, and a decent selection of beers. Casual. Meals
range from $6.95 to $11.95.
*Open Mon. - Thurs. 11 a.m. - 1 a.m., Fri. - Sat. 11 a.m. - 2 a.m.,
Sun. 11 a.m. - 12 a.m.*

Jimmy's Place
640 W. Northwest Hwy.
847/398-9783
Another popular hangout among locals, noted for cold beers and
cheap eats. They boast about their barbecued ribs for good reason,
and the pizza is always a good bet. Prices range from $5.95 to $10.95.
Open daily 10:30 a.m. - 10 p.m.

Vail Street Café
19 N. Vail Ave.
847/392-1164
The Vail Street is a gem, not so much because of the large bagels
and variety of coffees (all are good), but because of the owners'

support of the local art scene. Original art fills the walls on a rotating basis, weekends feature live music and poetry readings, and they've recently ventured into theater presentations. The café is a cultural favorite, and is likely to be even more popular as the downtown Arlington Heights renovation is completed.

Open daily 6 a.m. - 3 p.m. Call for evening performance hours.

Barrington

Penny Road Pub
164 Old Sutton Rd.
847/428-0562
Ask a local for directions to this friendly little out-of-the way neighborhood bar with a hard-rock jukebox and attitude to match. On weekends you'll often find live music, but more often you'll just find good company and a surprising menu that boasts almost a dozen different burgers. Nothing on the menu is more than $10.

Open Mon. - Sat. 10:30 a.m. - 4 a.m. Closed Sun.

RSVP's
333 W. Northwest Hwy.
847/381-5530
Once upon a time, this was a bar attached to a bowling alley. Now the alley is gone, but the bar and a small kitchen survive. In my early reporter and editor days, this was where I went to wind down and talk stories with the locals. Lunch prices are generally well under $10.

Open Mon. - Thurs. 10 a.m. - 12 a.m., Fri. - Sat. 10 a.m. - 2 a.m. Closing hours may vary depending on crowd. Closed Sun.

Yankee Doodle Inn
Behind Village Liquors on Main St.
847/381-1098
Like RSVP's (above), this friendly bar seems a little out of place in a town like Barrington. The interior is dim and generally smoky, but the inexpensive drinks and friendly atmosphere, along with its convenient proximity to the Barrington train station, continue to draw a "regulars" kind of crowd.

Open Mon. - Sat. 9 a.m. - 1 a.m., Sun. 11 a.m. - 9:30 p.m.

Elk Grove Village

Espresso Brewery Company II
958 Elk Grove Town Center
847/718-9272
This is a particularly welcome addition to the area's nightlife because there just aren't many places like it. If you're looking for coffee or tea and a light dessert, along with a helping of quality jazz, this is the place to be. Usually no cover charge.
Open Mon. - Thurs. 6 a.m. - 10 p.m., Fri. 6 a.m. - 12 a.m., Sat. 8 a.m. - 12 a.m., Sun. 8 a.m. - 8 p.m.

Hoffman Estates

North Beach Club
1001 N. Roselle Rd.
847/885-7030
Just about every indoor game you can think of can be played here, including sand volleyball. Draws a great and very fun crowd. Live music on Thursdays, DJ on Fridays and Saturdays.
Open Mon. - Thurs. 4 p.m. - 1 a.m., Fri. 4 p.m. - 2 a.m., Sat. 5 p.m. - 2 a.m. Closed Sun.

Island Lake

Mother Murphy's
213 E. State Rd.
847/526-8800
One of the most popular after-hours spots in and on the shores of Island Lake.
Open daily 3 p.m. - ?

Libertyville

Mickey Finn's
412 N. Milwaukee Ave.
847/362-6688
Mickey Finn's has a strangely wonderful personality, with microbrews, a lively crowd and staff, and a menu that ranges from great burgers to Mexican delights. Anywhere else and the menu might be called

schizophrenic. Prices are dirt cheap ($5-$11), though you'll likely spend a fin or two on the great brews.

Open Mon. - Thurs. 11 a.m. - 12 a.m. (full menu until 10 p.m., pizzas until 11 p.m.); Fri. - Sat. 11 a.m. - 1 a.m. (full menu until 11 p.m., pizzas until 12 a.m.); Sun. 12 p.m. - 9 p.m.

Lincolnshire

Flatlander's Restaurant and Brewery
Olde Half Day Rd. and Milwaukee Ave.
847/821-1234
There's always something worth hearing here, whether it be pop, rock, blues, or jazz. Most bands are quite good, especially considering the cover is $3-$5. And the beers flow easily; better take a cab.

Open for lunch Mon. - Fri. 11:30 a.m. - 2:30 p.m., Sat. 12 p.m. - 2:30 p.m., Sun. brunch 10 a.m. - 2 p.m.; for dinner Mon. - Thurs. 4:30 p.m. - 10:30 p.m., Fri. 4:30 p.m. - 11 p.m., Sat. 3:30 p.m. - 11 p.m., Sun. 3:30 p.m. - 10 p.m.

Long Grove

Village Tavern
135 McHenry Rd.
847/634-3117
It would be difficult to find a restaurant anywhere quite like the Village Tavern. The food (roadhouse-style burgers, meat-and-potatoes dinners) and service (always with a smile) are great, in spite of the large number of people who visit every day. Prices are very affordable ($5.95-$14.95), and the tavern portion of the large restaurant can be a welcome respite from a long day of shopping. Then again, everything here—antiques and collectibles line the walls—is for sale. Don't miss the enormous grandfather clock in the bar or the weekly auctions.

Kitchen open Mon. 11:30 a.m. - 9 p.m., Tues. - Sun. 11:30 a.m. - 10 p.m.; bar open daily 11:30 a.m. - 12 a.m.

Mount Prospect

Dumas Walker's
1799 S. Busse Rd.
847/593-2200
Mount Prospect meets Texas in this enormous country bar and eatery.
This is the only place east of the Mississippi with a dance floor the size
of a football field...and with enough friendly faces to fill it. Even if
you don't know how to line dance, you can learn how to here without
feeling like a fool. Weekends can be crowded—Dumas Walker's seems
to have come out of the country craze as a true survivor.
*Open Mon. - Thurs. 11 a.m. - 1 a.m., Fri. 11 a.m. - 2 a.m., Sat. 4 p.m. -
2 a.m., Sun. 4 p.m. - 10 p.m.*

Mrs. P and Me
100 E. Prospect Ave.
847/259-9724
This family-owned favorite has everything going for it. The interior is
casual and comfortable, the staff is friendly as can be, the American
food is always reliable, and prices won't bowl you over. (Few entrees
fall above $10.) On weekends, the focus shifts from the restaurant to
the bar, where you'll find plenty of friendly locals willing to tip a drink
or two.
*Kitchen open Mon. - Thurs. 11 a.m. - 9:30 p.m., Fri. - Sat. 11 a.m. -
10:30 p.m., Sun. 12 p.m. - 10 p.m.; bar open Mon. - Thurs. until
1 a.m., Fri. - Sat. until 2 a.m.*

Ye Olde Town Inn
18 W. Busse Ave.
847/392-3750
It's fair to say that if the locals aren't at Mrs. P & Me (see above
listing), they're either here or in bed. Ye Olde Town Inn has a slightly
more limited bar menu, but that's made up for in atmosphere and live
music on weekends. Food is impossibly cheap; just try to beat the 16-
oz porterhouse for $4.95 (honest) and complimentary appetizers from
4 p.m. to 6 p.m. Dart boards (cork and electronic) and pool tables stay
full on weekends. This is the kind of place that regulars don't want
anyone else to know about.
*Open Mon. - Thurs. 12 p.m. - 1 a.m., Fri. 12 p.m. - 2 a.m., Sat. 3 p.m. -
2 a.m., Sun. 3 p.m. - 9 p.m.*

Mundelein

The Annex
Rt.s 45 and 83
847/566-4400
There's food, but that's not what people come here for. Mostly it's the music, dancing, and single patrons consuming beverages.
Open Mon. - Fri. 11 a.m. - 11 p.m., Fri. - Sat. 11 a.m. - 12 a.m., Sun. 7 a.m. (for breakfast) - 10 p.m.

Gilmer Road House
25792 Midlothian Rd.
847/438-0300
Although easy enough to find, the Gilmer Road House is definitely off the beaten track. The pub-like décor is cozy, the people (customers and staff) are friendly, and the food is good, fast, and inexpensive. Most things fall under $10.
Open Mon. - Sat. 11 a.m. - 12 a.m., Sun. 8 p.m. - 10 p.m.

Uptown Saloon
26226 Rt. 60/83
847/949-7900
A very popular night spot in the area, the Uptown Saloon is fun when blues and pop acts perform, but it's an absolute riot on karaoke nights, which vary.
Open Sun. - Thurs. 11:30 a.m. - 1 a.m., Fri. - Sat. 11:30 a.m. - 2 a.m.

Palatine

Burning Ambitions Smoke Shop and Cigar Bar
19 N. Bothwell St.
847/358-0200
Tons of cigars to choose from in a very nice and distinctive atmosphere that still allows casual dress. My second-favorite spot for a good cigar. Open mic nights on Wednesdays are almost always a good time; believe it or not, a number of the brave souls who venture on stage have some talent.
Open Mon. - Thurs. 11 a.m. - 12 a.m., Fri. - Sat. 11 a.m. - 1 a.m. Closed Sun.

Slice of Chicago
36 S. Northwest Hwy.
847/991-2150
The type of music at Slice of Chicago varies from Chicago blues to pop rock, but the acts are always quality. Good Italian and American food is available in front; the back is where the action is and where you'll pay a low cover (usually $5 or less) for the entertainment.
Open Sun. - Thurs. 11 a.m. - 3 a.m., Fri. - Sat. 11 a.m. - 4 a.m.

Durty Nellie's West Irish Pub
55 N. Bothwell St.
847/358-9150
Around since 1972, Nellie's is hands-down one of the best venues for music in the 'burbs. It's also home to an incredible St. Patrick's Day party; something like 2,000 people moved through the doors on March 14, 1999. Music ranges from Celtic acoustic to rock and alternative; often two bands are playing at one time in different rooms. Covers are generally $5 or less. Open mic night on Mondays.
Open Sun. - Thurs. 11 a.m. - 1 a.m., Fri. - Sat. 11 a.m. -3 a.m.

Rolling Meadows

McGee's Bar and Grill
3425 Kirchoff Rd.
847/392-6446
The food and atmosphere of this friendly little spot brings in a good crowd of locals every night. Food is a little better than average pub grub, with most items under $10.
Open Sun. - Thurs. 11 a.m. - 2 a.m., Fri. - Sat. 11 a.m. - 3 a.m.

Rockhouse Grill
2212 Algonquin Rd.
847/392-6446
Another great venue for more contemporary rock, primarily from local and college bands. Cover is usually $4 or less.
Open Sun. - Thurs. 11 a.m. - 2 a.m., Fri. - Sat. 11 a.m. - 3:30 a.m.

Schaumburg

Alumni Club
871 E. Algonquin Rd.
847/397-3100
An enormous bar with televisions for sports events and a dance floor (DJs only). Typical clients tend to be post-college and upwardly mobile single professionals.
Open Sun. - Thurs. 11 a.m. - 1 a.m., Fri. - Sat. 11 a.m. - 3 a.m.

Corner Bakery
1901 E. Woodfield Rd.
847/240-1111
If it's just dessert and coffee you're after, the Corner Bakery is the place to go. The light sandwiches, bagels, breads, and sweets are delicious, though prices can be a bit high. That fact doesn't keep anyone away, however. There always seems to be a line.
Open for food Sun. - Thurs. 8 a.m. - 8 p.m., Fri. - Sat. 8 a.m. - 9 p.m.; for coffee and desserts until 9 p.m. and 10 p.m.

Easy Street Pub
17 S. Roselle Rd.
847/985-1366
Cold beer, great pizza, bar games, and friendly people. What more could you ask for on a Friday night?
Open Mon. - Thurs. 10:30 a.m. - 1 a.m., Fri. - Sat. 10:30 a.m. - 3 a.m., Sun. 10:30 a.m. - 12 a.m.

The Living Room
1850 E. Golf Rd. (next to the Hyatt Hotel)
847/330-1199
The food served upstairs at this upscale nightclub is very good, though the noise from the band downstairs may be a bit distracting on weekends after 9 p.m. Still, the crowd, which is mostly 35-and-over executives and business travelers, is friendly and the cigar selection is outstanding. Talk to the always charismatic Lee Kaboshi about renting your own humidor space near the stylish bar, or just share a cognac and friendly conversation.
Open Tues. - Thurs. 3 p.m. - 1 a.m., Fri. - Sat. 3 p.m. - 6 a.m. Closed Sun. - Mon.

Vernon Hills

Baja Beach Club
285 Center Dr.
847/573-1602
By night it's a dance club/cigar bar for the 21-and-over (but not by much) crowd. On Sundays in summer it turns into a popular juice bar for teens.
Open Wed. 8 p.m. - 1 a.m., Fri. - Sat. 8 p.m. - 2 a.m., Sun. (June-Aug.) 5 p.m. - 10:30 p.m. (teens only). Closed Mon., Tues., & Thurs.

Legends Sports Bar & Grill
102 E. Hawthorn Pkwy.
847/680-4300
Food, ballgames, pool tables, and video games make this the penultimate sports bar for the north-central Lake County crowd.
Closed for remodeling. Call for hours..

Zanies Comedy Club
230 Hawthorn Village Commons
847/549-6030
Need a laugh? Zanies has 'em in droves. Usually the stand-up comics are from the local circuit, but top names from Hollywood, including Richard Lewis, have also brought the house down. There is a two-beverage minimum, but most people don't have too much of a problem meeting that. Prices aren't gouging.

Wheeling

Crawdaddy Bayou
412 N. Milwaukee Ave.
847/520-4800
After a trip or two to New Orleans, I developed a fondness for Southern cooking, mudbugs, and Zydeco music. Since then, Crawdaddy Bayou in Wheeling substantially reduced my road-trip time. All of the above, and more, can be found inside these swamp-themed walls. This is one of my favorite places to just kick back and hang out, especially when there's a band in the bar Thursday through Sunday.
Open for lunch Tues. - Sun. 11:30 a.m. - 2:30 p.m.; for dinner Tues. - Thurs. 5 p.m. - 10 p.m., Fri. - Sat. 5 p.m. - 11 p.m., Sun. 4 p.m. - 9 p.m. Closed Mon.

94th Aero Squadron
1070 S. Milwaukee Ave.
847/459-3700
If you're in the mood for dancing in a unique environment, in this case, one decorated with airplane memorabilia, the 94th Aero Squadron, on the edges of Palwaukee Airport, is the place. A balanced menu of American fare is available, and the combination of food and music make this is a popular place for singles groups.
Open for lunch Mon. - Fri. 11:30 a.m. - 2:30 p.m.; for dinner Sun. - Thurs. 4 p.m. - 10 p.m., Fri. - Sat. 4 p.m. - 12 a.m.; for dancing Fri. - Sat. until 2 a.m.

SOLO EXPEDITIONS

Singles Groups

There are a number of very active singles organizations throughout the suburbs, many geared toward specific age groups or religious and cultural interests. Several churches and synagogues, listed in individual village chapters also offer groups and meeting places for singles. Call for information.

Attachments, Inc.
630/584-1031
Dance parties and other events at various locations in the far Northwest Suburbs.

Christian Singles (Ages 50+)
Calvary Temple
450 Keller Ave.
Waukegan
847/244-1632
This non-denominational group open to all adult singles in far North Suburbs, including Mundelein, Libertyville, and Vernon Hills, meets weekly.

Colossal Social Club
847/604-3404
Group designed for what they refer to as "plus-size people" meets twice monthly throughout the area.

Helpmates of Elk Grove
Lutheran Church of the Holy Spirit
150 Lions Dr.
Elk Grove Village
847/437-5897
Includes Bible study groups and support for widowed, separated, and divorced people from Elk Grove Village and surrounding suburbs.

Holy Family Phoenix Ministry
Holy Family Catholic Church
2515 Palatine Rd.
Inverness
847/359-0042
A non-denominational group offering programs and support for
the widowed, separated, divorced, and remarried. Small donation
requested at meetings.

Jewish Social Singles
847/579-0755
Restaurant socials and various events scheduled almost weekly
throughout the North and Northwest Suburbs.

New Beginnings
Hubert's Church
729 Grand Canyon St.
Hoffman Estates
847/885-7700
Catholic-oriented support group for widowed, separated, and divorced
people.

North Shore Jewish Singles (Ages 50+)
847/674-6798
Various events for adult singles in North and Near-northwest Suburbs.

Solo Singles
Gale Street Inn
906 Diamond Lake Rd.
Mundelein
847/746-6818
Weekly meetings for all singles include dancing and socializing. Free
admission.

Single Parent Network of Lake Forest
847/604-3446
Social and support programs for single parents 35 and over in the
North and Northwest Suburbs.

Thunderbird Singles
847/604-3446
Various dance parties offered almost weekly to all singles in Arlington

Heights, Schaumburg, and surrounding suburbs.

Young Single Parents
Arlington Park Hilton
3400 W. Euclid St.
Arlington Heights
847/818-3339
Various support and social activities offered to single parents, including those divorced, widowed, and separated.

SHOP 'TIL YOU DROP

Mall Mania (Shopping Centers)

Something Old, Something Cool
(Antiques)

Reading Material (Bookstores)

The entrance to Yaohan Plaza—a Japanese shopping mall in Arlington Heights.

The fruits of Yaohan Plaza in Arlingon Heights.

MALL MANIA

Almost every village in the Northwest Suburbs has something to boast about in terms of retail shopping, but if you need to hit a lot of stores at one time, the local malls are the places to go.

Woodfield Mall
Woodfield Rd. just west of Rt. 53
Schaumburg
847/330-1537
Woodfield Mall is one of the largest shopping malls in the world, and you'll know it the moment you step into any of the entrances. More than 280 stores line the maze of hallways and ramps; you'll want to grab a map at the information desk located in the center of the mall to avoid getting lost. Many of the stores are high-end (Nordstrom, Marshall Field's, etc.), but there's always a sale going on somewhere. There are several decent restaurants in the mall (see *Schaumburg*, pp. 154 - 155, for specifics), and a movie theater as well. Although the parking lot is enormous, you'll not often find an empty space close to any of the entrances. Expect a long walk, or consider an investment in valet parking.
Open Mon. - Fri. 10 a.m. - 9 p.m., Sat. 10 a.m. - 7 p.m., Sun. 11 a.m. - 6 p.m. Hours vary during holiday shopping seasons. Directions: Take I-90 to Rt. 53; go south on Rt. 53 to Woodfield Rd.; go west on Woodfield Rd. to first stoplight. Woodfield Mall is on the right.

Streets of Woodfield
Woodfield Rd. just west of Rt. 53
Schaumburg
847/995-9700 (Mid-American Real Estate, Mon. - Fri. 9 a.m. - 5 p.m.)
Just across the street from Woodfield Mall, even more shopping awaits those who just can't get enough. The Streets of Woodfield is still under development. In its original guise as "One Schaumburg Place," most of the retail shops went bust. Village officials and area developers made a significant effort to turn things around, and it seems to be working. Galyan's, an enormous sporting goods store, is one of the primary anchors and it alone is worth a visit, if only to give the climbing wall a

try. Just outside the mall, but on the same property, The Corner Bakery and Maggiano's Little Italy are two exceptional reasons to avoid shopping at all.
Directions: Take I-90 to Rt. 53; go south on Rt. 53 to Woodfield Rd.; go west on Woodfield Rd. to first stoplight. Streets of Woodfield is on the left.

Randhurst Shopping Center
Rand Rd. (Rt. 12) and Elmhurst Rd. (Rt. 83)
999 N. Elmhurst Rd.
Mount Prospect
847/259-0500
Randhurst Shopping Center l is much smaller than Woodfield, but because of that, it's also generally less crowded. The selection of stores is still decent—with department stores like Carson Pirie Scott, Sears, and Ward's; and the mall itself is much easier to navigate. There are several fast-food chains in the mall if you need a quick bite, but for a decent restaurant, you'll have to leave the premises.
Open Mon. - Fri. 10 a.m. - 9 p.m., Sat. 10 a.m. - 7 p.m., Sun. 11 a.m. - 6 p.m. Hours vary during holiday shopping seasons. Directions (from Chicago): Take I-90 west to Elmhurst Rd. exit; take Elmhurst Rd. north to Rand Rd. Randhurst Shopping Center will be on the right.

Hawthorne Center
Milwaukee Rd. (Rt. 21) and Town Line Rd. (Rt. 60)
122 Hawthorne Center
Vernon Hills
847/362-6220
With 150 stores offering everything from clothes and jewelry to travel services and eyewear, Hawthorne Square is pretty much the one-stop spot for residents living north of Lake-Cook Road. It's a large, open mall with a comfortable layout. Decent bargains can be found at stores like Eddie Bauer and Ward's almost any time of year, but expect some serious crowds around Christmas. Your best choices for dining lay outside the mall, as the food court is made up strictly of fast-food chains.
Open Mon. - Fri. 10 a.m. - 9 p.m., Sat. 10 a.m. - 7 p.m., Sun. 11 a.m. - 6 p.m. Hours vary during holiday shopping seasons. Directions: Take I-94 to Town Line Rd. (Rt. 60); take Rt. 60 west, just past Milwaukee Rd. Hawthorne Center is on the right.

Yaohan Plaza
Northeast corner of Algonquin and Arlington Heights roads
Arlington Heights
Designed primarily to cater to the large Japanese and Japanese-American population of the Northwest Suburbs, Yaohan Plaza is an intriguing place for people of any ethnicity to shop. You'll find few other places offering sashimi-quality fresh fish next to daikon radishes, pickled scallions, and lemon grass. But Yaohan is not simply a grocery store; the compact mall features shops where you can purchase anything from Japanese serving dishes, some of which are very affordable, to Japanese greeting cards. A small food court offers a simple range of dishes at reasonable prices, and if you're on the run, you can even pick up some just-packaged sushi or a bento box to go.
Directions: Take I-90 to Arlington Heights Rd.; go north on Arlington Heights Rd. about a half-mile. The entrance to Yaohan Plaza is on the right.

Village of Long Grove
Rt. 83 and Robert Parker Coffin Rd.
847/634-9440 (Village Hall)
The Village of Long Grove has nothing to do with "mall shopping," but we'd be remiss if we didn't clue you into one of the nicest shopping experiences around. The quaint streets of Long Grove are brimming with specialty shops, antique stores, and art galleries, and in peak season, there are plenty of tourists wandering through them. Don't let that stop you. Parking is free in the center of downtown, and on a nice summer day a visit to Long Grove can be a panacea of sorts. Various festivals are held year-round (don't miss the Strawberry Festival), and you'll also want to check out the Long Grove Confectionery Company for a pound or two of homemade chocolate.
Directions: Take I-294 north to Lake-Cook Rd.; take Lake-Cook Rd. west to Rt. 83; take Rt. 83 north to Robert Parker Coffin Rd.; turn left and follow signs to Historic Village of Long Grove. Stores open daily 10 a.m. - 5 p.m., but may vary with the seasons.

Visitors wander through downtown Long Grove, a good spot for antique shoppers.

SOMETHING OLD, SOMETHING COOL

ANTIQUE SHOPPING

Arlington Heights

All My Treasures
7 E. Miner St.
847/394-2944

Arlington Antique Shoppe
1139 S. Arlington Heights Rd.
847/439-1778

Arlington Antiques Etc.
208 N. Dunton Ave.
847/788-1481

Cobblestone Antiques
17 E. Miner St.
847/259-4818

The Collage Antiques
1005 S. Arlington Heights Rd.
847/439-5253

Oakton Street Antique Center
2430 E. Oakton Ave.
847/437-2514

P.J.'s Antiques and Collectibles
116 N. Evergreen Ave.
847/259-7130

Barrington

Jan's of London
200 Applebee St.
847/381-5767

Romantiques
118 W. Main St.
847/304-8582

Buffalo Grove

The Best of Times
847/279-1093
Call for appointment.

Des Plaines

Pace Auctions
794 Lee St.
847/296-0773

Lake Zurich

The Antique Shop
247 N. Rand Rd.
847/540-0500

Lincolnshire

Rebecca Anne Antiques
23346 N. Milwaukee Ave.
847/634-2423

Long Grove

Artistic Illusion Custom Antiques
317 Old McHenry Rd.
847/478-9401

Carriage Trade Interiors
425 Robert Parker Coffin Rd.
847/634-3160

Emporium of Long Grove
227 Robert Parker Coffin Rd.
847/634-0188

Especially Maine Antiques
Robert Parker Coffin Rd.
847/634-3512

Mrs. B & Me
132 Old McHenry Rd.
847/634-7352

Palatine

Anne's Unique Boutique II
60 W. Illinois Ave.
847/963-1976

Wauconda

Country Casual Antiques
109 S. Main St.
847/526-7880

Liberty Antiques
201 N. Main St.
847/487-1764

Tin Horse Antiques
451 W. Liberty St.
847/487-7973

Whippletree Farm Antiques
210 S. Main St.
847/526-7808

Wheeling

The Coach House Antiques
971 N. Milwaukee Ave.
847/808-1324

County Faire Inc.
971 N. Milwaukee Ave.
847/537-9987

O'Kelly's Antiques
971 N. Milwaukee Ave.
847/537-1656

READING MATERIAL

Arlington Heights

Crown Books (chain)
430 E. Rand Rd.
847/577-1003
Large selection of various titles at discount prices.

Dawn's Christian Books & Music (independent)
832 E. Rand Rd.
847/788-9600
Religious books, bibles, and church supplies.

Drummer & Thumbs New & Used Books (independent)
1 E. Campbell St.
847/398-8968
A book lover's paradise, with shelves upon shelves (and stacks
upon stacks) of used books in all genres at substantial discounts.
Small selection of new titles and rare books.

Victoria's Books Ltd. (independent)
13 W. Campbell St.
847/788-1313
High-quality used and collectible books, including many antiquarian
first editions and autographed books.

Lake Zurich

B. Dalton Bookseller (chain)
Lake Zurich Shopping Center
847/438-0112
Large selection of new titles in all genres.

Crown Books (chain)
795 W. Main St.
847/438-6166

Libertyville

Marytown Press and Marytown Catholic Gift Shop (independent)
1600 W. Park Ave.
847/367-7800
Religious books, bibles, and church supplies.

Long Grove

Mad About Books (independent)
324 Old McHenry Rd.
847/478-1059
Eclectic selection of top-quality used and rare books.

Mount Prospect

Jack's Used Books (independent)
718 E. Northwest Hwy.
847/398-7767
A very large and well-organized selection of quality used and rare books in good condition.

Kroch's & Brentano's (independent)
Randhurst Shopping Center
847/259-5510
Large selection of new titles in all genres.

Prairie Moon Ltd. (independent)
864 E. Northwest Hwy.
847/342-9608
Unique and fascinating selection of feminist books in a "woman-friendly" space.

Palatine

Beyond Tomorrow Science Fiction Books & Comics (independent)
327 N. Northwest Hwy.
847/705-6633
This is the place for sci-fi buffs to find everything from Asimov to
Zelazny.

The Christian Shop, Ltd. (independent)
2070 Rand Rd.
847/991-8994
Religious books, bibles, and gifts.

Schaumburg

Barnes & Noble Booksellers (chain)
590 E. Golf Rd.
847/310-0450
Enormous selection of new titles and periodicals in all genres, in
a comfortable, reader-friendly atmosphere. Small café on site.

Border's Books & Music (chain)
1540 E. Golf Rd.
847/330-0031
Enormous selection of new books in all genres. Also features a large
collection of music titles.

Doubleday Book Shop (chain)
Woodfield Mall
847/330-1514
Large selection of new titles in all genres.

Rand McNally Map & Travel (chain)
Woodfield Mall
847/995-9606
Large selection of maps, atlases, and travel-related books.

Waldenbooks/Waldenkids (chain)
Woodfield Mall
847/619-6850
Large selection of new titles in all genres.

Vernon Hills

Bookids (chain)
402 Hawthorn Center
847/918-8160
Large selection of books and educational material geared toward young children.

Crown Books (chain)
701 Milwaukee Ave.
847/816-1421

Wauconda

Laura's Pennywise Paperbacks (independent)
115 S. Main St.
847/487-0106

RECREATIONAL PURSUITS

The Great Outdoors
(Forest Preserves and Great America)

Native Links (Golfing)

Strike Zones (Bowling Alleys)

Bakers Lake in Barrington.

THE GREAT OUTDOORS

The Forest Preserves

Nature is never very far away when you visit the Northwest Suburbs. All of the towns in this book are served by either the Cook County or Lake County forest preserve districts.

The Lake County Forest Preserves are a collection of about a dozen large sites specifically designed for recreational use. One of the largest preserves is home to the Lake County Museum.

The Cook County Forest Preserve District offers at least as many large sites, most of which have picnic tables and places to toss a Frisbee.

Each location offers miles and miles of hiking and biking trails, and many also have horseback riding and snowmobile trails. Free maps can be obtained at the forest preserves' general offices listed below.

Lake County Forest Preserve District
2000 N. Milwaukee Ave.
Libertyville
847/367-6640

Cook County Forest Preserve District
536 N. Harlem Ave.
River Forest
708/366-9420

Lake County Museum and Lakewood Forest Preserve
Rt. 176 and Fairfield Rd.
Wauconda
847/526-7878
The Lake County Museum is a small but eclectically thorough place

where you can find everything from the natural history of northern Illinois to local art and artifacts. The most curious collection is certainly the Curut Teich Postcard Archives, which features literally hundreds of thousands of postcards created by the Curt Teich Company of Chicago between 1898 and 1978. While artistically interesting enough to bear a visit, the postcards actually serve as a visual history of advertising and industrial development throughout the 20th century. *Open Mon. - Sat. 11 a.m. - 4:30 p.m., Sun. 1 p.m. - 4:30 p.m. Admission $2.50 for adults, $1 for children; free on Tues.*

Ryerson Conservation Area
(part of the Lake County Forest Preserve system)
21950 N. Riverwoods Rd.
Deerfield
847/948-7750
Whether you like bird watching, biking, or just a quiet stroll through the woods, the Edward L. Ryerson Conservation Area, a.k.a. Ryerson Woods, is the place to be.

More than half of the 550-acre site is officially designated as an Illinois Nature Preserve for the sake of protecting a variety of endangered and rare flora and fauna native to northern Illinois. The preserve is home to a number of rare species ranging from the spotted salamander to the red-shouldered hawk.

The central building houses a large library containing books on the natural sciences and a children's resource center. Special events and nature programs are offered year-round.
Open daily 6:30 a.m. - 5 p.m. Visitors center open daily 9 a.m. - 5 p.m.

Crabtree Nature Center
Palatine Rd. west of Barrington Rd.
Barrington Hills
This is the place to be in spring, when birds are migrating and flowers are blooming. It's a wonderful place just to walk as well, but don't miss the educational aspects of the trip. A great place to bring kids on a sunny day.

Amusement Parks

Six Flags Great America Theme Park
I-94 and Rt. 132
Gurnee
847/249-1776
The largest theme park in Illinois, Great America is located just north of the Libertyville/Mundelein/Vernon Hills area on I-94. The park features a number of impressive roller coasters, along with dozens of rides, games, and concession stands.
Open on weekends only late Apr. - mid-May & Sept. - Oct. Daily hours mid-May - late Aug. Admission $36 for adults, with half-price discounts available for seniors and some children (height-based requirements); free for children under 2 years.

NATIVE LINKS

The many public golf courses in the Northwest Suburbs range from beginner- to pro-level. Many are in very scenic, peaceful settings, and for the most part are quite affordable. While there are a number of courses from which to choose, golfers are abundant, so you're best advised to make your tee times as far in advance as possible.

Golf programs at area high schools are quite popular, so during the summer you'll likely share the course with young teenagers, and the performance quality of both teens and adults varies widely. A few courses, such as Rob Roy in Prospect Heights, have age restrictions. Bring a healthy dose of patience, observe the course rules (most now require soft spikes on golf shoes, and some are considering dress codes), and you'll be rewarded with an enjoyable day on the links.

Price Key (for 18 holes at peak times)
$ – dirt cheap (less than $15)
$$ – still a bargain ($15 to $30)
$$$ – better be decent ($30 to $60)
$$$$ – time to turn pro ($60+)

Arlington Heights

Arlington Lakes
1211 S. New Wilke Rd.
847/577-3030
This par-68 course offers a few challenges for the novice duffer, including several water holes, more than 100 bunkers, and the infamous ninth hole, which features an intimidating approach over water, some nasty bunkers, and a meanly-sloped green. Limited café available.
Twilight rates available. **$$**

Nickol Knoll
3800 N. Kennicott Dr.
847/590-6050
Surprising challenges can be found on this par-27, nine-hole course, which features some hilly approaches and attractive natural roughs. Prices also make this spot particularly attractive for a short afternoon round. Small pro shop.
Twilight rates available. $$

Barrington

Barrington Park District
235 Lyons Rd.
847/381-0687
If you only have an hour during your lunch and want to punch a few, this is the place to come. There are only ten holes and no tee times are necessary. The cheap fee also makes it a great place to learn or teach the game without worrying about the quality of the players around you.
$

Thunderbird Country Club
(open to the public)
1010 E. Northwest Hwy.
847/381-6500
Thunderbird Country Club is a very nice, sprawling par-71 course in a beautiful setting. Challenges include several water holes and deep bunkers, along with a couple of long fairways and holes that will test your accuracy. Blue tees play at about 6,169 yards. The clubhouse features a restaurant and bar, as well as a large pro shop.
Twilight rates available. $$

Buffalo Grove

Buffalo Grove Golf Course
48 Raupp Blvd.
847/537-5819
This par-72 course has enough challenges for players of every level, with the longest blue tees playing at about 6,892 yards. The front nine features an often tricky ninth hole, but the real beauty starts at the deceptive tenth fairway. There is a driving range and practice greens. The clubhouse offers a large pro shop, along with a full restaurant and

bar. One of the most popular golf courses measured by rounds per season in the country.
Twilight rates available after 4 p.m. **$$**

Arboretum Golf Course
401 Half Day Rd.
847/913-1112
This is Buffalo Grove's newest golf course and is really a gem for the serious golfer. There's a challenge on almost every hole; most are narrow, and 15 holes feature water hazards. Long tees play at 6,477 yards on the par-72 course. Prices are a little steeper here.
Twilight rates available after 4 p.m. **$$$**

Des Plaines

Lake Park
2222 Birch St.
847/391-5730
There's not much to this par-54, 18-hole course, but it makes for a pleasant afternoon outing when you don't have a lot of time, and fees are dirt cheap. A popular destination for seniors and families, especially on weekends.
$

Elk Grove Village

Fox Run
533 Plum Grove Rd.
847/228-3544
This par-70 course isn't too demanding, but it has enough challenges to keep the day interesting. Try to fit in 18 so you can visit the signature number ten hole.
Twilight rates available after 3 p.m. **$$**

Fox Lake

Fox Lake Golf Course
7220 State Park Rd.
847/587-6411
It's worth the short drive north of Island Lake to visit this stellar and

challenging golf course. The longest tees play at 6,347 yards (par-72 course), but what the course lacks in length it makes up for in precision and beauty. A good iron game is essential here, and you'd best brush up on your putting skills before facing the rolling greens.
$$$

Hoffman Estates

Highland Woods
2775 N. Ela Rd.
847/991-0950
Highland Woods is a nice course with reasonable challenges, but nothing too intimidating unless you consider the 6,995 yards you'll travel from the first long tee to the last. There are only six water holes, but they're tough, and the more than 50 bunkers will keep you on your toes. Lighted driving range. Clubhouse features a large pro shop and small snack shop.
Twilight rates available after 4 p.m. *$$*

Hilldale Golf Course
1625 Ardwick Dr.
847/310-1100
Robert Trent Jones Sr. designed this par-71 course that measures 6,434 yards from top to bottom. Challenging enough for pros, so come with your A-game. Carts are mandatory during certain times of day; the hills make it worth the investment, anyway.
Twilight rates available. *$$$*

Poplar Creek Golf Course
1400 Poplar Creek Dr.
847/781-3681
Not terribly long at 6,108 yards from the longest tees, but the majority of holes offer a water threat, and there's sand everywhere. The Hoffman Estates Park District operates a golf dome here during winter months for the die-hard golfer, and there is a full restaurant and bar open in summer months. All in all a pleasant afternoon for the money.
Twilight rates available. *$$$*

Libertyville

Riverside Park
870 Country Club Rd.
847/362-5733
A par-27, nine-hole course strictly for beginners and golfers who need a quick lunch-time fix. Small pro shop, mostly for last-minute needs.
$

Lincolnshire

Marriott's Lincolnshire Resort Golf Course
10 Marriott Dr.
847/634-5935
A par-70 course that plays at 6,313 yards from end to end. This is not only one of the most scenic courses around, it's also one of the most fun. Greens are surrounded by beach, and water comes into play frequently. The resort has two restaurants and a wonderful lounge where live music can be heard most weekend evenings. The clubhouse offers a complete pro shop.
Twilight rates available. $$$

Long Grove

Kemper Lakes
Old McHenry Rd.
847/320-3450
The jewel of a par-72 course of northern Illinois has played host to such events as the PGA Championship, the U.S. Women's Championship, and the Ameritech Senior Open. A lovely, demanding course, it consistently ranks as one of the top 100 courses in the nation by writers in the know. Prices, of course, reflect that stellar image. Championship tees play at 7,217 yards (blue tees are at 6,680 yards).
$$$$

Mount Prospect

Mount Prospect Golf Course
600 S. See-Gwun Ave.
847/632-9300
Like many of the area's park district-owned golf courses, Mount Prospect Golf Course began as a private course. The par-71 course dates back to the 1950s, so there are a number of mature trees and thick grasses to get in the way of errant shots. Small greens and lots of water give plenty of challenges, but the pleasant design and layout ease away worries.
Twilight rates available after 3:30 p.m. $$$

Old Orchard Country Club
(open to the public)
700 W. Rand Rd.
847/255-2025
A really sharp-looking course, maintained to perfection. The fairways feel like carpeting beneath your feet. About ten holes feature water, and there aren't quite as many bunkers as other area courses, but they're big. In general, the course is really pleasant. The clubhouse features an outdoor grill with a decent menu.
$$$

Mundelein

Countryside Golf Course
20800 W. Hawley St.
847/566-5544
Countryside offers two par-72 courses: the West Course is the oldest in Lake County, created in the mid-1920s as a private course for Samuel Insull. There are fewer water holes and bunkers on the West Course, but it has more character. The East Course plays longer, at 6,757 yards from the long tees.
Twilight rates available. $$

Four Winds
23110 W. Highway 176
847/566-8502
A complete pro shop, driving range, and golf school make this a great place to get started. The course has enough teeth for most better-than-

average golfers. Fairways and greens are maintained nicely.
Twilight rates available after 4 p.m. $$$

Indian Valley
Routes 45 and 83
847/566-1313
For a par-72 course, Indian Valley plays relatively short, at 5,988
yards. But it's a very affordable course and a nice place to spend
a morning or afternoon.
Twilight rates after 4 p.m. weekdays, 3 p.m. weekends. $$

Pine Meadow
One Pine Meadow Ln.
847/566-4653
This one is a toughie, but if you can beat it you'll remember the day for
a long time. Tournament tees measure 7,141 yards from end to end
(regular tees hit 6,450 yards). Golf publications consistently rank this
course among the top in the nation for its water, sand, and length. A
course that demands patience, placement, and persistence.
Twilight rates available. $$$

Steeple Chase
200 N. La Vista Dr.
847/949-8900
Steeple Chase's roller-coaster greens will leave you scratching your
head for the perfect line, and there are some moderate challenges along
the fairways in bunkers and water. The course offers a complete pro
shop and decent prices.
Twilight rates available after 3 p.m. $$$

Village Green
2501 N. Midlothian Rd.
847/566-7373
Village Green is not terribly demanding, but it is popular among area
players for its par-70, 6,235-yard distance and playability, especially
early in the season when you're just getting your game in gear. Prices
can't be beat. The complete pro shop is a good place to stock up on
golf balls.
Twilight rates available after 3 p.m. weekdays, 4 p.m. weekends. $$

Palatine

Palatine Hills Golf Course
512 W. Northwest Hwy.
847/359-4020
Length is probably the most intimidating factor at this par-72, 6,800-yard course. The driving range is a good place to warm up, and the clubhouse offers a small pro shop. Prices make this a popular destination for locals looking for a quick break.
Ttwilight rates available after 4 p.m. $$

Twin Lakes
1200 E. Lake Dr.
847/934-6050
There are some nice surprises on this well-designed and well-maintained par-29, nine-hole course, beginning with the very first hole. Prices, along with a complete pro shop and driving range, make this a favorite destination for beginners and teenagers looking to sharpen their games.
$

Prospect Heights

Rob Roy Golf Course
505 E. Camp McDonald Rd.
847/253-4544
Long and narrow fairways are challenge enough; then throw in the condos, town homes, and single-family dwellings and you've got the par-36 Rob Roy. Fortunately, the course designers figured there were enough obstacles without throwing in more than a handful of water holes and bunkers. Prices are quite affordable, and there is a limited pro shop and bar/snack shop. This is a "sleeper" course that never seems to be swarming with people. Some age restrictions apply; call for details.
$

Schaumburg

Schaumburg Golf Course
401 N. Roselle Rd.
847/885-9000
There's always a little mystery at this marvelous 27-hole gem; the pro staff alternates the combination of holes between the par-72 "championship course" and the nine-hole "player's course." Fairways are beautifully maintained, and the course, which was built in the late 1920s, features mature trees and tons of character. There's plenty here to challenge any level of player.
$$

Walnut Greens
1150 Walnut Ln.
847/490-7878
Walnut Greens is an enjoyable little par-3 course designed with families in mind. Children 9-11 years old may play if accompanied by adults, and family rates are available. You can bet families take advantage of this spot; a game here is less than the cost of a movie.
$

Streamwood

Streamwood Oaks
565 Madison Dr.
708/483-1881
The nine holes at Streamwood Oaks have enough challenges for a course twice the size, and that makes it a favorite among area golfers. *This course has a dress code. Call for details. $$*

Vernon Hills

Vernon Hills Public Golf Course
291 Evergreen Dr.
847/680-9310
They've recently put some money into the greens and clubhouse of this nine-hole, par-34 golf course and it shows. There isn't too much drama here, but you'll find enough challenges to keep your game sharp.
$

Wheeling

Chevy Chase Golf Course
1000 N. Milwaukee Ave.
847/537-0082
Lots of water, lots of sand, lots of distance. All of your skills will be put to the test at this beautiful, older golf course. The European lodge-style clubhouse has a complete pro shop and is a very popular spot for banquets and wedding receptions (read: crowded parking lot on weekends). The par-72 course measures 6,721 yards from end to end. *Twilight rates available.* **$$**

STRIKE ZONES

Arlington Heights

Arlington Heights Lanes
3435 N. Kennicott Ave.
847/255-6373

Beverly Lanes
8 S. Beverly Ln.
847/253-5238

Des Plaines

Des Plaines Bowling Lanes
656 Pearson St.
847/299-2862

Elk Grove Village

Elk Grove Bowl
Higgins and Arlington Heights roads
847/437-3395

Hoffman Estates

Hoffman Lanes
80 W. Higgins Rd.
847/885-2500

Poplar Creek Bowl
2354 W. Higgins Rd.
847/310-9585

Island Lake

3D Bowling Lanes & Sideouts Bar
Roberts Rd. and Rt. 176
847/526-7174

Lake Zurich

Bear's Country Sports Pub & Lanes
561 W. Main St.
847/438-7231

Mount Prospect

Thunderbird Lanes
821 E. Rand Rd.
847/392-0550

Palatine

Brunswick Northwest Bowl
519 S. Consumer Ave.
847/392-8290

Rolling Meadows

AMF Bowling Centers
3245 Kirchoff Rd.
847/259-4400

Schaumburg

Woodfield Lanes
350 E. Golf Rd.
847/843-2300

Vernon Hills

Hawthorn Lanes
316 Center Dr.
847/367-1600

Wauconda

Wauconda Bowl
381 W. Liberty St.
847/526-5030

Wheeling

Jeffery Lanes
125 N. Wolf Rd.
847/537-5370

BEDDING DOWN

Hotels and Motels

Entering the beautiful property of St. Mary's of the Lake in Mundelein.
Though you can't stay the night, this campus is one of
the Northwest Suburbs' most restful havens.

BEDDING DOWN

HOTELS AND MOTELS

Arlington Heights

Ambassador Monthly Suites
2423 N. Kennicott Dr.
847/398-3200

Amerisuites Chicago
211 S. Arlington Heights Rd.
847/956-1400

Arlington Park Hilton Hotel & Conference Center
3400 W. Euclid St.
847/394-2000

Best Western Arlington Inn
948 E. Northwest Hwy.
847/255-2900

Courtyard By Marriott
3700 N. Wilke Rd.
847/394-9999

Courtyard By Marriott
100 W. Algonquin Rd.
847/437-3344

Holiday Inn
2120 S. Arlington Heights Rd.
847/593-9400

Keyes Motel
2323 E. Rand Rd.
847/253-2003

La Quinta Inn
1415 W. Dundee Rd.
847/253-8777

Motel 6
441 W. Algonquin Rd.
847/806-1230

Pines Motel
109 E. Rand Rd .
847/253-7258

Radisson Hotel
75 W. Algonquin Rd.
847/364-7600

Regal Hotels
1904 E. Waverly Ln.
847/818-0320

Barrington

Days Inn
405 W. Northwest Hwy.
847/381-2640

Buffalo Grove

Hilton Garden Inn
900 W. Lake-Cook Rd.
847/215-8883

Extended Stay Apartments
1525 Busch Pkwy.
847/215-0641

Deerfield

Embassy Suites Chicago North Shore
1445 Lake-Cook Rd.
847/945-4500

Residence Inn by Marriott
530 Lake-Cook Rd.
847/940-4644

Des Plaines

Club Hotel
1450 E. Touhy Ave.
847/296-8866

Comfort Inn
2175 E. Touhy Ave.
847/635-1300

Courtyard By Marriott
2950 S. River Rd.
847/824-7000

Drury Northwestern Motel
374 Lee St.
847/297-2018

Rand Manor Motel
1322 Rand Rd.
847/827-7447

Travelodge Chicago-O'Hare
3003 Mannheim Rd., #201
847/296-5541

Elk Grove Village

Ambassador Monthly Suites
480 Eagle Dr., #101
847/517-8890

Best Western Inn
1600 Oakton St.
847/981-0010

Comfort Inn
2550 Landmeier Rd.
847/364-6200

Days Inn
1920 E. Higgins Rd.
847/593-6460

Elk Grove Motel
2325 E. Higgins Rd.
847/437-0820

Excel Inn of O'Hare
2881 Touhy Ave.
847/803-9400

Excel Inn
1000 W. Devon Ave.
847/895-2085

Hampton Inn
100 Busse Rd.
847/593-8600

Holiday Inn
1000 Busse Rd.
847/437-6010

La Quinta Inn
1900 Oakton St.
847/439-6767

Motel 6
1601 Oakton St.
847/981-9766

Hoffman Estates

Budgetel Inn
2075 Barrington Rd.
847/882-8848

Hampton Inn & Suites
2825 Greenspoint Pkwy.
847/882-4301

La Quinta Inn
2280 Barrington Rd.
847/882-3312

Red Roof Inn
2500 Hassell Rd.
847/885-7877

Libertyville

Newcastle Hotel
522 N. Milwaukee Ave.
847/367-9876

Best Inns Of America Motel
1809 N. Milwaukee Ave.
847/816-8006

Best Western Hitch-Inn Post
1765 N. Milwaukee Ave.
847/362-8700

Doe's Motel
31228 N. U.S. Rt. 45
847/362-0800

Lincolnshire

Courtyard By Marriott
505 Milwaukee Ave.
847/634-9555

Hampton Inn & Suites
1400 Milwaukee Ave.
847/478-1400

Hawthorn Suites Hotel
10 Westminster Way
847/945-9300

Marriott's Lincolnshire Resort
10 Marriott Dr.
847/634-5935

Mount Prospect

Ramada Inn
200 E. Rand Rd.
847/255-8800

Mundelein

Holiday Inn
510 E. Rt. 83
847/949-5100

Ramada Inn
517 E. Rt. 83
847/566-5400

Super 8 Motel
1950 S. Lake St.
847/949-8842

Northbrook

Sybaris Inn
3350 Milwaukee Ave.
847/298-5000

Hilton Inn
2855 Milwaukee Ave.
847/480-7500

Radisson Hotel
2875 Milwaukee Ave.
847/298-2525

O'Hare Airport

See also "Rosemont" listings, p. 285.

O'Hare Hilton
O'Hare International Airport
Chicago
773/686-8000

Wyndham Garden Hotel
5615 N. Cumberland Ave.
Chicago
773/693-5800

Palatine

Bel Air Motel
536 E. Northwest Hwy.
847/358-0100

Haven Motel
600 E. Northwest Hwy.
847/358-0020

Holiday Inn
1550 E. Dundee Rd.
847/934-4900

Motel 6
1450 E. Dundee Rd.
847/359-0046

Ramada Woodfield Hotel
920 E. Northwest Hwy.
847/359-6900

Rand Motel
20393 N. Rand Rd.
847/438-8288

Prospect Heights

Forest Lodge
1246 River Rd.
847/537-2000

Excel Inn of Prospect Heights
540 N. Milwaukee Ave.
847/459-0545

Rolling Meadows

Comfort Inn Rolling Meadows
2801 Algonquin Rd.
847/259-5900

Extended Stay America
2400 Golf Rd.
847/357-1000

Motel 6
1800 Winnetka Cir.
847/818-8088

Rosemont

Best Western Inn
10300 W. Higgins Rd.
847/296-4471

Clarion International
6810 N. Mannheim Rd.
847/297-8464

Holiday Inn
5440 N. River Rd.
847/671-6350

Hotel Sofitel
5550 N. River Rd.
847/678-4488

Hyatt Hotels & Resorts
9300 Bryn Mawr Ave.
847/696-1234

Marriott Hotels & Resorts
6155 N. River Rd.
847/696-4400

Quality Inn
6810 Mannheim Rd.
847/297-1234

Ramada Inn
6600 Mannheim Rd.
847/827-5131

Rosemont Suites
5500 N. River Rd.
847/678-4000

Sheraton Gateway Suites
6501 N. Mannheim Rd.
847/699-6300

Westin Hotel O'Hare
6100 N. River Rd.
847/698-6000

Schaumburg

Amerisuites Hotel
1851 McConnor Pkwy.
847/330-1060

Amerisuites Hotel
2750 Greenspoint Pkwy.
847/839-1800

Bowman's Woodfield Corporate
475 N. Martingale Rd.
847/517-8890

Chicago Marriott Schaumburg
50 N. Martingale Rd.
847/240-0100

Country Inn & Suites
1401 N. Roselle Rd.
847/839-1010

Drury Inns
600 N. Martingale Rd.
847/517-7737

Embassy Suites Hotel
1939 N. Meacham Rd.
847/397-1313

Hampton Inn
1300 E. Higgins Rd.
847/619-1000

Holiday Inn
1550 N. Roselle Rd.
847/310-0500

Homewood Suites
815 E. American Ln.
847/605-0400

Hyatt Regency Woodfield
1800 E. Golf Rd.
847/605-0328

La Quinta Inn
1730 E. Higgins Rd.
847/517-8484

Marriott Hotels & Resorts
50 N. Martingale Rd.
847/240-0100

Radisson Hotel
1725 E. Algonquin Rd.
847/397-1500

Summerfield Suites
901 E. Woodfield Office Ct.
847/619-6677

Wyndham Garden Hotel Schaumburg
800 National Pkwy.
847/605-9222

Vernon Hills

Amerisuites
450 Milwaukee Ave.
847/918-1400

Wauconda

Wauconda Motel
26671 N. U.S. Rt. 12
847/526-2101

Wheeling

Olde Court Inn
374 N. Milwaukee Ave.
847/537-2800

Palwaukee Motor Inn
1090 S. Milwaukee Ave.
847/537-9100

Wishing Well Motel
397 N. Milwaukee Ave.
847/537-3590

EVERYTHING ELSE

Getting To Know You
(Community Organizations)

To Your Health (Hospitals)

Going Postal (Post Offices)

County Chiefs (Contact Information)

Inverness's pastoral village hall.

GETTING TO KNOW YOU

Selected Community Organizations

Alcoholism-Drug Dependence (ADD) Program
Lutheran Social Services Behavioral Health Program
4811 Emerson Ave., Ste. 112
Palatine
847/397-0095

Alliance Against Intoxicated Motorists
870 E. Higgins Rd., #131
Schaumburg
847/240-0027
Advocates for victims, and families of victims, of drunken driving incidents.

American Association of Retired Persons (AARP)
Prairie Lakes Community Center
515 E. Thacker St.
Des Plaines
847/391-5717

AARP Chapter 2255
793 Beach Pl.
Mundelein
847/566-1767

American Red Cross
544 W. Northwest Hwy.
Arlington Heights
847/255-0703

Audubon Society, Lake County
206 W. Maple Ave.
Libertyville
847/362-7053

Bicycle Club of Lake County
P.O. Box 521
Libertyville
847/604-0520

Boy Scouts of America
2745 Skokie Valley Rd.
Highland Park
847/433-1813

Camera Club of Lake County
419 Northgate Rd.
Lindenhurst
847/566-1373

Catholic Charities
33 S. Arlington Heights Rd.
Arlington Heights
847/253-5500

Center of Concern
1580 N. Northwest Hwy.
Park Ridge
847/823-0453

Children's Advocacy Center of Northwest Cook County
640 Illinois Blvd.
Hoffman Estates
847/885-0100
Intervention, education, and prevention programs related to child sexual abuse.

Citizens for Conservation
211 N. Ela Rd.
Barrington
847/382-7283

Clearbrook Center
2800 W. Central Rd.
Rolling Meadows
847/870-7711

**Community and Economic Development
Association of Cook County, Inc.**
CEDA Northwest Self Help Center
120 W. Eastman Ct.
Arlington Heights
847/392-2332
Nutrition programs for children and seniors, as well as housing assistance, programs for the homeless, budget and employment counseling, energy services, emergency assistance, Head Start, and day care assistance.

Countryside Association
21154 W. Shirley Rd.
Palatine
847/438-8855

Des Plaines Camera Club
820 Graceland Ave., #303
Des Plaines
847/696-2899

Des Plaines Valley Geological Society
214 N. Broadway Ave.
Park Ridge
847/823-0634

Greater Woodfield Convention and Visitors Bureau
1375 E. Woodfield Rd., Ste. 100
Schaumburg
847/605-1010

The Heartland Institute
800 E. Northwest Hwy., Ste. 1080
Palatine
847/202-3060

Home of the Sparrow
1509 N. Oak St.
Palatine
847/963-8030

Hospice of Northeastern Illinois
410 S. Hager Ave.
Barrington
847/381-5599
Medicare-certified hospice program serving terminally ill patients and providing grief support for families of the terminally ill.

Kenneth Young Centers
1001 Rohlwing Rd.
Elk Grove Village
847/529-8800

Kenneth Young Center for Senior Services
2500 W. Higgins Rd., Ste. 655
Hoffman Estates
847/885-1631

Kid's Line (telephone help line)
P.O. Box 1321
Elk Grove Village
847/228-5437
24-hour help line for children 13 years old and under.

Lake County Forest Preserves
2000 N. Milwaukee Ave.
Libertyville
847/367-6640

Lake County Services
847/360-6600

League of Women Voters
209 W. Fremont St.
Arlington Heights
847/392-6195

Life Span
P.O. Box 445
Des Plaines
847/824-0382

LifeSource Blood Center
1145 N. Roselle Rd.
Hoffman Estates
847/884-7766

Literacy Volunteers of America
200 N. Grove Ave.
Elgin
847/742-6565
Confidential assistance and training for functionally illiterate people of all ages.

National Association for Uniformed Service
22 Manchester Ct.
Streamwood
630/289-0921
Non-profit veterans organization providing advocacy and lobbyists for welfare and benefits issues.

Northern Illinois Business Association
625 N. Court, Ste. 300
Palatine
847/963-9860

Northwest Action Against Rape
415 W. Golf Rd., Ste. 47
Arlington Heights
847/228-0990
Support agency for victims of sexual assault and their families and partners.

Northwest Cultural Council
P.O. Box 690
Barrington
847/956-7966
Offers various arts- and writing-related workshops, as well as an art gallery with frequent juried shows.

Northwest Mental Health Center
1616 N. Arlington Heights Rd.
Arlington Heights
847/392-1420

Northwest Suburban Association of Commerce and Industry (NSACI)
1450 E. American Ln., Ste. 140
Schaumburg
847/517-7110

Northwest Symphony Orchestra Association, Inc.
1603 E. Thacker St.
Des Plaines
847/317-9343

Omni Youth Services
1616 N. Arlington Heights Rd.
Arlington Heights
847/253-6010

Parents Who Care
P.O. Box 68631
Hoffman Estates
630/483-0637

Public Action to Deliver Service (PADS)
525 W. Higgins Rd., Ste. 205
Schaumburg
847/843-3933

Rainbow Hospice, Inc.
1550 N. Northwest Hwy., #220
Park Ridge
847/699-2000

Resource Center for the Elderly
306 W. Park St.
Arlington Heights
847/577-7070
A local, not-for-profit organization that creates training programs and housing options to help keep elderly residents in their homes.

The Salvation Army Community Counseling Center
609 W. Dempster St.
Des Plaines
847/981-9113

25 Illinois Blvd.
Hoffman Estates
847/885-4060

Shelter, Inc.
1616 N. Arlington Heights Rd.
Arlington Heights
847/255-8060
Emergency and temporary housing for abused and neglected children up to the age of 17.

Talk Line (telephone help line)
847/228-6400
24-hour help line for adults, offering crisis intervention and support.

Teen Line (telephone help line)
847/228-8336
24-hour support and counseling for teenagers 13 and older.

United Way
308 N. Evergreen Ave.
Arlington Heights
847/259-2007

Women In Need Growing Stronger (WINGS)
P.O. Box 53
Park Ridge
847/803-2537
Provides assistance to homeless and abused single women and single mothers in the North and Northwest Suburbs.

Woodfield Area Charity Organization
1901 N. Roselle Rd., Ste. 800
Schaumburg
847/490-5946

A toast to the Biloxi Grill of Wauconda: It's good for your health!

TO YOUR HEALTH

Arlington Heights

Northwest Community Hospital
800 W. Central Rd.   847/618-1000

Barrington

Good Shepherd Hospital—Advocate
450 W. Highway 22   847/381-9600

Des Plaines

Holy Family Hospital
100 N. River Rd.   847/297-1800

Elgin

St. Joseph Hospital
77 Airlite St.   847/695-3200

Sherman Hospital
934 Center St.   847/742-9800

Elk Grove Village

Alexian Brothers Medical Center
800 Biesterfield Rd.   847/437-3397

Glenview

Glenbrook Hospital
2100 Pfingsten Rd.   847/657-5800

Highland Park

Highland Park Hospital
718 Glenview Rd.   847/432-8000

Hoffman Estates

Columbia Hoffman Estates Medical Center
1555 N. Barrington Rd.   847/843-2000

Libertyville

Condell Medical Center
801 S. Milwaukee Ave.   847/362-2900

Park Ridge

Lutheran General Hospital
1775 Dempster St.   847/723-2210

GOING POSTAL

Northwest Suburban Post Offices

Arlington Heights
909 W. Euclid Ave.
Arlington Heights, IL 60005   847/253-7456

Barrington
1515 S. Grove Ave.
Barrington, IL 60010   847/381-0514

106 Barrington Commons
Barrington, IL 60010

Buffalo Grove
255 N. Buffalo Grove Rd.
Buffalo Grove, IL 60089   847/520-0089

Des Plaines
1000 East Oakton St.
Des Plaines, IL 60018   847/827-5591

Elk Grove Village
611 Landmeier Rd.
Elk Grove Village, IL 60007   847/439-5573

Hoffman Estates
1255 N. Gannon Dr.
Hoffman Estates, IL 60195   847/885-6510

Island Lake
129 E. State Rd.
Island Lake, IL 60042   847/526-6153

Lake Zurich
380 Surryse Rd.
Lake Zurich, IL 60047   847/438-2460

Libertyville
1520 Artaius Pkwy.
Libertyville, IL 60048   847/362-2266

675 Lakeview Pkwy.
Libertyville, IL 60048   847/566-3900

Lincolnshire
230 Northgate St.
Lake Forest, IL 60045   847/234-0654

Mount Prospect
300 W. Central Rd.
Mount Prospect, IL 60056   847/392-2730

Mundelein
435 E. Hawley St.
Mundelein, IL 60060   847/566-7167

Palatine
440 W. Colfax St.
Palatine, IL 60067   847/359-1791

Prospect Heights
9 S. Elmhurst Rd.
Prospect Heights, IL 60070   847/255-1770

Rolling Meadows
3266 Kirchoff Rd.
Rolling Meadows, IL 60008   847/255-8474

Schaumburg
450 W. Schaumburg Rd.
Schaumburg, IL 60194   847/885-6500

Streamwood
115 E. Irving Park Rd.
Streamwood, IL 60107   630/837-5488

Vernon Hills
422 Hawthorne Center
Vernon Hills, IL 60061   847/367-5335

Wauconda
539 W. Liberty St.
Wauconda, IL 60084   847/526-7111

Wheeling
250 W. Dundee Rd.
Wheeling, IL 60090   847/537-0700

Construction in the downtown area of Arlington Heights
will bring new retail shops and condominiums.

COUNTY CHIEFS

Cook County Government

Cook County Assessor's Office
118 N. Clark St., Rm. 537
Chicago, IL 60602   312/443-5300

Cook County County Board
118 N. Clark St., Rm. 537
Chicago, IL 60602   312/443-6396

Cook County Clerk's Office
118 N. Clark St., Rm. 434
Chicago, IL 60602   312/443-7891

Cook County Forest Preserve District
50 W. Washington St., # 307
Chicago, IL 60602   312/443-6555

Cook County Sheriff's Office
50 W. Washington St., # 704
Chicago, IL 60602   312/443-4521

Lake County Government

Lake County Assessor's Office
18 N. County St.
Waukegan, IL 60085   847/360-6378

Lake County Board
18 N. County St.
Waukegan, IL 60085   847/360-6336

Lake County Clerk's Office
18 N. County St.
Waukegan, IL 60085   847/360-3610

Lake County Forest Preserve District
2000 N. Milwaukee Ave.
Libertyville, IL 60048   847/367-6640

Lake County Sheriff's Office
25 S. Utica St.
Waukegan, IL 60085   847/360-6300

INDEX

T

ABOUT THE AUTHOR

Martin A. Bartels

is a journalist and free-lance travel writer whose work has appeared in numerous publications, including the *Jerusalem Post*, the *Greenville News* (South Carolina), and the 53 papers of suburban Chicago's Pioneer Press Newspapers, Inc.

Both music and literature were inseparable parts of Bartels' childhood. In addition to being a writer, he is a songwriter whose first instrumental jazz composition, "No Need to Trouble Yourself," debuted on Waukegan's WKRS-AM radio in April 1999.

Born in a northern suburb of Chicago, Bartels moved to the mountains of Colorado at the age of seven. He remained there until he graduated from college in 1982, when he returned to the Chicago area to pursue a career in journalism. As a community news reporter, news editor, and entertainment editor at Pioneer Press, he has covered more than 20 suburban villages, many of which he has also called home.

Bartels' interests in wine, music, food, and culture make him a natural for travel writing. As a freelance writer, he has traveled extensively to locales including Italy, Southern France, Central America, the Eastern Caribbean, Mexico, Hawaii, Alaska, and 20 of the "lower 48" states.

He lives in the Chicago area with his wife, Robin, where he is working on a screenplay and a novel.

PUBLISHER'S CREDITS

Cover Design by Timothy Kocher.

Interior Design by Sharon Woodhouse.

Cover Photos by Martin A. Bartels.

Photos by Martin A. Bartels.

Photo Captions by Martin A. Bartels and Sharon Woodhouse.

Maps by Bill Lane.

Editing by Bruce Clorfene.

Proofreading by Brandon Zamora, Sharon Woodhouse, Susan McNulty, Ken Woodhouse, and Brandei Bell.

Layout by Brandon Zamora and Sharon Woodhouse.

Indexing by Brandon Zamora and Sharon Woodhouse.

The text of *A Native's Guide To Chicago's Northwest Suburbs* was set in Times New Roman, with headers in CAC Norm Heavy.

LAKE CLAREMONT PRESS FAVORITES

Chicago Haunts: Ghostlore of the Windy City (Revised Edition)
by Ursula Bielski
From ruthless gangsters to restless mail order kings, from the Fort Dearborn Massacre to the St. Valentine's Day Massacre, the phantom remains of the passionate people and volatile events of Chicago history have made the Second City second to none in the annals of American ghostlore. Bielski captures over 160 years of this haunted history with her unique blend of lively storytelling, in-depth historical research, exclusive interviews, and insights from parapsychology. Called "a masterpiece of the genre," "a must-read," and "an absolutely first-rate-book" by reviewers, *Chicago Haunts* continues to earn the praise of critics and readers alike.
0-9642426-7-2, October 1998, softcover, 277 pages, 29 photos, $15

Hollywood on Lake Michigan: 100 Years of Chicago and the Movies
by Arnie Bernstein
This engaging history and street guide finally gives Chicago and Chicagoans due credit for their prominent role in moviemaking history, from the silent era to the present. With trivia, special articles, historic and contemporary photos, film profiles, anecdotes, and exclusive interviews with dozens of personalities, including Studs Terkel, Roger Ebert, Gene Siskel, Dennis Franz, Harold Ramis, Joe Mantegna, Bill Kurtis, Irma Hall, and Tim Kazurinsky. Foreword by *Soul Food* writer/director, George Tillman, Jr.
0-9642426-2-1, December 1998, softcover, 364 pages, 80 photos and graphics, $15

Know More, Spend Less: A Native's Guide To Chicago, 3rd Edition
by Sharon Woodhouse,
with expanded South Side coverage by Mary McNulty
Venture into the nooks and crannies of everyday Chicago with this unique, comprehensive budget guide. Over 400 pages of free, inexpensive, and unusual things to do in the Windy City make this the perfect resource for tourists, business travelers, visiting suburbanites, and resident Chicagoans.
0-9642426-0-5, January 1999, softcover, 438 pages, photos, maps, $12.95

Whether you're a life-long resident, new in town, or just passing through, let the *Native's Guide* series for Chicago's suburban regions be your personal tour guides of the best our suburbs have to offer.

A Native's Guide to Chicago's Northern Suburbs
by Jason Fargo
Historic homes, forts, churches, cemeteries, chamber music, Bach Week , outdoor concerts, award-winning theater, celebrated museums, hiking, biking, canoeing, bocce ball, bowling, golf, beaches, water parks, lagoons, nature centers, botanical gardens, four star restaurants, delis, coffeehouses, lunch counters, ethnic banquet halls, French pastries, pizza, Korean BBQ, charhouse chops, tapas, tamales, caviar & Cognac, Ravinia, discos, elegant lounges, cigar salons, billiards, roadside pubs, college football, landmark movie houses, mega-malls, quaint corner stores, chocalatiers, dairymarts, mystery bookstores, handmade pottery, art fairs, food feasts, Oktoberfests, winter carnivals, comedy workshops, and much more!
0-9642426-8-0, June 1999, softcover, 207 pages, photos, maps, $12.95

A Native's Guide to Chicago's Western Suburbs
by Laura Mazzuca Toops and John W. Toops, Jr.
The Underground Railroad, Ernest Hemingway, Frank Lloyd Wright masterpieces, Sears Catalog homes, restored prairies, sprawling estates, corporate headquarters, cemeteries, Brookfield Zoo, antiques, boutiques, Harley-Davidson mall, Old World bakeries, candy counters, hearty Bohemian, haute French, hot Mexican, sushi, Tiki bars, microbreweries, golf, polo, race tracks, trolley tours, equestrian trails, ice rinks, orchestras, ballet, movie palaces, dinner theater, laser shows, Kiddieland, wine bars, folk music, coffee houses, county fairs, and much more!
0-9642426-6-4, August 1999, softcover, 210 pages, photos, maps, $12.95

A Native's Guide to Chicago's South Suburbs
by Christina Bultinck and Christy Johnston-Czarnecki
Forts, cemeteries, parks, trails, art galleries, architecture, ghostly tales, ice cream parlors, bakeries, brunch, steakhouses, pizza, ribs, chili, race tracks, country clubs, sports bars, dance halls, casinos, biking, fishing, horseback riding, sledding, mega-malls, antiques, boutiques, collectibles, crafters, car shows, trivia, Who's Who, "We're #1, We're #1!", and much more!
0-9642426-1-3, June 1999, softcover, 242 pages, photos, maps, $12.95

Full of the fascinating sights, places, stories, and facts that sometimes even locals don't know about, the *Native's Guide* series equips you with everything you need to enjoy and navigate Chicago's suburbs like a true insider.

ORDER FORM

Please send me autographed copies of the following Lake Claremont Press titles:

A Native's Guide to Chicago, 3rd Ed.　　　_____ @ $12.95 = _____

A Native's Guide To Chicago's
South Suburbs　　　_____ @ $12.95 = _____

A Native's Guide To Chicago's
Northern Suburbs　　　_____ @ $12.95 = _____

A Native's Guide To Chicago's
Western Suburbs　　　_____ @ $12.95 = _____

**A Native's Guide To Chicago's
Northwest Suburbs**　　　_____ @ $12.95 = _____

Chicago Haunts: Ghostlore of
the Windy City, Revised Ed.　　　_____ @ $15.00 = _____

Hollywood on Lake Michigan:
100 Years of Chicago & The Movies　　　_____ @ $15.00 = _____

Subtotal: _____

**Discounts when you order
multiple copies!**

2 books—10% off total
3-4 books —20% off total
5-9 books—25% off total
10+ books—40% off total

Less Discount: _____

New Subtotal: _____
8.75% tax for
Illinois Residents: _____

Shipping Fees

$2 for the first book and
$.50 for each additional
book or a maximum of $5.

Shipping: _____

TOTAL: _____

Name_____

Address_____

City_____**State**_____**Zip**_____

Please enclose check, money order, or credit card number.

Visa/Mastercard#_____**Exp.** _____

Signature_____

Lake Claremont Press
P.O. Box 25291
Chicago, IL 60625
773/784-7517, 773/784-6504 (fx)
LakeClarPr@aol.com

Order by mail, phone, fax, or e-mail.
*All of our books have a no-hassle, 100%
money back guarantee.*

MORE CHICAGO BOOKS FROM LAKE CLAREMONT PRESS

Know More, Spend Less: A Native's Guide To Chicago, 3rd Edition
by Sharon Woodhouse
with expanded South Side coverage by Mary McNulty

A Native's Guide To Chicago's South Suburbs
by Christina Bultinck and Christy Johnston-Czarnecki

A Native's Guide To Chicago's Northern Suburbs
by Jason Fargo

A Native's Guide To Chicago's Western Suburbs
by Laura Mazzuca Toops and John W. Toops, Jr.

Chicago Haunts: Ghostlore of the Windy City
by Ursula Bielski

*Hollywood on Lake Michigan:
100 Years of Chicago and the Movies*
by Arnie Bernstein

COMING SOON

Graveyards of Chicago
by Matt Hucke and Ursula Bielski

Chicago Resource Guide for the Chronically Ill and Disabled
by Susan McNulty

Literary Chicago: A Book Lover's Tour of the Windy City
by Gregory Holden